# CouchDB and PHP Web Development Beginner's Guide

Get your PHP application from conception to deployment by leveraging CouchDB's robust features

**Tim Juravich**

BIRMINGHAM - MUMBAI

# CouchDB and PHP Web Development Beginner's Guide

Copyright © 2012 Packt Publishing

First published: June 2012

Production Reference: 1150612

Published by Packt Publishing Ltd.
Livery Place
35 Livery Street
Birmingham B3 2PB, UK.

ISBN 978-1-849513-58-6

www.packtpub.com

Cover Image by Parag Kadam (paragvkadam@gmail.com)

# Credits

**Author**
Tim Juravich

**Reviewers**
Gonzalo Ayuso

David Carr

Wenbert Del Rosario

**Acquisition Editor**
Sarah Cullington

**Lead Technical Editors**
Arun Nadar

Chris Rodrigues

**Technical Editor**
Lubna Shaikh

**Project Coordinator**
Leena Purkait

**Proofreader**
Kevin McGowan

**Indexer**
Monica Ajmera Mehta

**Graphics**
Manu Joseph

Valentina D'silva

**Production Coordinator**
Arvindkumar Gupta

**Cover Work**
Arvindkumar Gupta

# About the Author

**Tim Juravich** is an experienced product, program, and technology leader who has spent the past decade leading teams through a variety of projects in PHP, Ruby, and .NET. After gaining experience at several Fortune 500 companies, Tim discovered entrepreneurship, founded three of his own startups, and helped dozens of other startups open their doors.

Tim currently serves as the Director of Program Management for Thinktiv, a venture accelerator. When not at work, Tim actively mentors engineers, contributes to open source projects, and works on a variety of side projects.

Check out Tim's blog at `http://juravich.com`, and be sure to follow him on Twitter `@timjuravich`

I would like to thank my loving parents, my older (but smaller) brother Jon, and my wife Leigha. Without Leigha's support and love through our first year of marriage, this book, and much more, would not have been possible.

I would also like to thank my clients and colleagues who have provided invaluable opportunities for me to shape my career, my life, and my perspective on technology.

# About the Reviewers

**Gonzalo Ayuso** is a web architect with more than 10 years of experience in web development, specializing in open source technologies. He has experience in delivering scalable, secure, and high-performing web solutions to large scale enterprise clients. He has a varied background, always related to Linux and the Internet. He is mainly focused on Internet technologies, databases, and programming languages (mostly PHP, Python, and JavaScript). You can check his blog at gonzalo123.wordpress.com or follow him on Twitter @gonzalo123.

**Wenbert Del Rosario** is from Cebu, Philippines. He started his career as a web developer in college, learning PHP and Adobe Photoshop. He works with open source technologies – Zend Framework, Code Igniter, MySQL, jQuery, and Wordpress are some of the tools he has up his sleeve. He also works with Django (Python) and Ruby on Rails.

In his free time, he loves to work on personal projects. He also does some freelance and consulting. He knows he has a lot to learn, but his experience has taught him to solve real-world and business problems. He is very passionate and shares some of his thoughts and day-to-day encounters through his blog (http://blog.ekini.net).

Wenbert's latest employer is Norwegian Pacific Offshore. He also has worked for Lexmark Research and Development Corporation in Cebu.

I would like to thank my family and my wife, Noeme, for all their support and encouragement.

# www.PacktPub.com

## Support files, eBooks, discount offers and more

You might want to visit www.PacktPub.com for support files and downloads related to your book.

Did you know that Packt offers eBook versions of every book published, with PDF and ePub files available? You can upgrade to the eBook version at www.PacktPub.com and as a print book customer, you are entitled to a discount on the eBook copy. Get in touch with us at service@packtpub.com for more details.

At www.PacktPub.com, you can also read a collection of free technical articles, sign up for a range of free newsletters and receive exclusive discounts and offers on Packt books and eBooks.

http://PacktLib.PacktPub.com

Do you need instant solutions to your IT questions? PacktLib is Packt's online digital book library. Here, you can access, read and search across Packt's entire library of books.

### Why Subscribe?

- ◆ Fully searchable across every book published by Packt
- ◆ Copy and paste, print and bookmark content
- ◆ On demand and accessible via web browser

### Free Access for Packt account holders

If you have an account with Packt at www.PacktPub.com, you can use this to access PacktLib today and view nine entirely free books. Simply use your login credentials for immediate access.

# Table of Contents

## Bonus Chapter

**You can download the Bonus Chapter from**
`http://www.packtpub.com/sites/default/files/downloads/Replicating_`
`your_Data.pdf.`

# Preface

PHP and CouchDB Web Development will teach you the fundamentals of combining CouchDB and PHP to create a full application from conception to deployment. This book will direct you in developing a basic social network, while guiding you through some of the common pitfalls that are frequently associated with NoSQL databases.

## What this book covers

*Chapter 1, Introduction to CouchDB,* provides a quick definition of NoSQL and an overview of CouchDB.

*Chapter 2, Setting up your Development Environment,* sets up your computer for developing an application with PHP and CouchDB.

*Chapter 3, Getting Started with CouchDB and Futon,* defines CouchDB documents and shows how to manage them both from the command-line and within Futon – CouchDB's built-in administration utility.

*Chapter 4, Starting your Application,* creates a simple PHP framework to house your application and publishes this code to GitHub.

*Chapter 5, Connecting your Application to CouchDB,* connects your application to CouchDB using a variety of methods, and ultimately picks the right solution for your application.

*Chapter 6, Modeling Users,* creates users within your application and handles document creation and authentication with CouchDB.

*Chapter 7, User Profiles and Modeling Posts,* perfects your user profile using Bootstrap and posts content to CouchDB.

*Chapter 8, Using Design Documents for Views and Validation,* explores CouchDB's exclusive use of Design Documents to improve the quality of your application.

*Chapter 9, Adding Bells and Whistles to your Application*, leverages existing tools to simplify and improve your application.

*Chapter 10, Deploying your Application*, shows your application to the world, and teaches you how to launch your application and database using a variety of Cloud services.

*Bonus Chapter, Replicating your Data*, finds out how to use CouchDB's replication system to scale your application as it grows.

You can download the *Bonus Chapter* from `http://www.packtpub.com/sites/ default/files/downloads/Replicating_your_Data.pdf`.

# What you need for this book

You'll need a modern computer with Mac OSX. *Chapter 1, Introduction to CouchDB,* will provide the setup instructions for Linux and Windows machines, and the code written in this book will work on any machine. However, the majority of the command-line statements and applications that we'll use in this book are Mac OSX-specific.

# Who this book is for

This book is for beginners and intermediate PHP developers, who are interested in using CouchDB development in their projects. Advanced PHP developers will appreciate the familiarity of the PHP architecture, and can easily learn how to incorporate CouchDB into their existing development experiences.

# Conventions

In this book, you will find several headings appearing frequently.

To give clear instructions of how to complete a procedure or task, we use:

## Time for action – heading

1. Action 1

2. Action 2

3. Action 3

Instructions often need some extra explanation so that they make sense, so they are followed with:

# What just happened?

This heading explains the working of tasks or instructions that you have just completed.

You will also find some other learning aids in the book, including:

## Pop quiz – heading

These are short multiple choice questions intended to help you test your own understanding.

## Have a go hero – heading

These set practical challenges and give you ideas for experimenting with what you have learned.

You will also find a number of styles of text that distinguish between different kinds of information. Here are some examples of these styles, and an explanation of their meaning.

Code words in text are shown as follows: " It's difficult to standardize the `install` methods for Linux, because there are many different flavors and configurations."

A block of code is set as follows:

```
<Directory />
  Options FollowSymLinks
  AllowOverride None
  Order deny,allow
  Allow from all
</Directory>
```

When we wish to draw your attention to a particular part of a code block, the relevant lines or items are set in bold:

```
<Directory />
  Options FollowSymLinks
  AllowOverride All
  Order deny,allow
  Allow from all
</Directory>
```

Any command-line input or output is written as follows:

```
sudo apt-get install php5 php5-dev libapache2-mod-php5 php5-curl php5-mcrypt
```

**New terms** and **important words** are shown in bold. Words that you see on the screen, in menus or dialog boxes for example, appear in the text like this: "Start by opening **Terminal**".

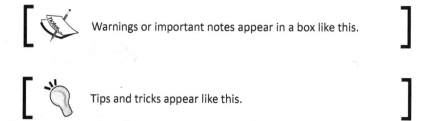

Warnings or important notes appear in a box like this.

Tips and tricks appear like this.

# Reader feedback

Feedback from our readers is always welcome. Let us know what you think about this book—what you liked or may have disliked. Reader feedback is important for us to develop titles that you really get the most out of.

To send us general feedback, simply send an e-mail to feedback@packtpub.com, and mention the book title through the subject of your message.

If there is a topic that you have expertise in and you are interested in either writing or contributing to a book, see our author guide on www.packtpub.com/authors.

# Customer support

Now that you are the proud owner of a Packt book, we have a number of things to help you to get the most from your purchase.

## Downloading the example code

You can download the example code files for all Packt books you have purchased from your account at http://www.packtpub.com. If you purchased this book elsewhere, you can visit http://www.packtpub.com/support and register to have the files e-mailed directly to you.

# Errata

Although we have taken every care to ensure the accuracy of our content, mistakes do happen. If you find a mistake in one of our books—maybe a mistake in the text or the code—we would be grateful if you would report this to us. By doing so, you can save other readers from frustration and help us improve subsequent versions of this book. If you find any errata, please report them by visiting http://www.packtpub.com/support, selecting your book, clicking on the **errata submission form** link, and entering the details of your errata. Once your errata are verified, your submission will be accepted and the errata will be uploaded to our website, or added to any list of existing errata, under the Errata section of that title.

# Piracy

Piracy of copyright material on the Internet is an ongoing problem across all media. At Packt, we take the protection of our copyright and licenses very seriously. If you come across any illegal copies of our works, in any form, on the Internet, please provide us with the location address or website name immediately so that we can pursue a remedy.

Please contact us at copyright@packtpub.com with a link to the suspected pirated material.

We appreciate your help in protecting our authors, and our ability to bring you valuable content.

# Questions

You can contact us at questions@packtpub.com if you are having a problem with any aspect of the book, and we will do our best to address it.

# 1
# Introduction to CouchDB

*Welcome to CouchDB and PHP Web Development Beginner's Guide. In this book, we will learn the ins and outs of building a simple but powerful website using CouchDB and PHP. For you to understand why we do certain things in CouchDB, it's first important for you to understand the history of NoSQL databases and learn CouchDB's place in database history.*

In this chapter we will:

- Go over a brief history of databases and their place in technology
- Talk about how databases evolved into the concept of NoSQL
- Define NoSQL databases by understanding different classifications of NoSQL databases, the CAP theorem and its avoidance of the ACID model
- Look at the history of CouchDB and its main contributors
- Talk about what makes CouchDB special

Let's start by looking at the evolution of databases and how NoSQL arrived on the scene.

## The NoSQL database evolution

In the early 1960s, the term **database** was introduced to the world as a simple layer that would serve as the backbone behind information systems. The simple concept of separating applications from data was new and exciting, and it opened up possibilities for applications to become more robust. At this point, databases existed first as tape-based devices, but soon became more usable as system direct-access storage on disks.

In 1970, Edgar Codd proposed a more efficient way of storing data – the relational model. This model would also use SQL to allow the applications to find the data stored within its tables. This relational model is nearly identical to what we know as traditional relational databases today. While this model was widely accepted, it wasn't until the mid 1980s that there was hardware that could actually make effective use of it. By 1990, hardware finally caught up, and the relational model became the dominant method for storing data.

Just as in any area of technology, competition arose with **Relational Database Management Systems (RDBMS)** . Some examples of popular RDMBS systems are Oracle, Microsoft SQL Server, MySQL, and PostgreSQL.

As we moved past the year 2000, applications began to produce incredible amounts of data through more complex applications. Social networks entered the scene. Companies wanted to make sense of the vast amounts of data that were available. This shift brought up some serious concerns about the datastructure, scalability, and availability of data that the relational model didn't seem to handle. With the uncertainty of how to manage this large amount of ever-changing data, the term NoSQL emerged.

The term **NoSQL** isn't short for "no SQL;" it actually stands for "not only SQL". NoSQL databases are a group of persistent solutions, which do not follow the relational model and do not use SQL for querying. On top of that, NoSQL wasn't introduced to replace relational databases. It was introduced to complement relational databases where they fell short.

# What makes NoSQL different

Besides the fact that NoSQL databases do not use SQL to query data, there are a few key characteristics of NoSQL databases. In order to understand these characteristics, we'll need to cover a lot of terminology and definitions. It's not important that you memorize or remember everything here, but it's important for you to know exactly what makes up a NoSQL database.

The first thing that makes NoSQL databases different is their data structure. There are a variety of different ways in which NoSQL databases are classified.

## Classification of NoSQL databases

NoSQL databases (for the most part) fit into four main data structures:

- **Key-value stores**: They save data with a unique key and a value. Their simplicity allow them to be incredibly fast and scale to enormous sizes.
- **Column stores**: They are similar to relational databases, but instead of storing records, they store all of the values for a column together in a stream.

- **Document stores**: They save data without it being structured in a schema, with buckets of key-value pairs inside a self-contained object. This datastructure is reminiscent of an associative array in PHP. This is where CouchDB lands on the playing field. We'll go much deeper into this topic in *Chapter 3, Getting Started with CouchDB and Futon.*

- **Graph databases**: They store data in a flexible graph model that contains a node for each object. Nodes have properties and relationships to other nodes.

We won't go too deeply into examples of each of these types of databases, but it's important to look at the different options that are out there. By looking at databases at this level, it's relatively easy for us to see (in general) how the data will scale to size and complexity, by looking at the following screenshot:

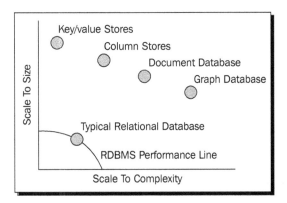

If you look at this diagram, you'll see that I've placed a **Typical Relational Database** with a crude performance line. This performance line gives you a simple idea of how a database might scale in size and complexity. How is it possible that NoSQL databases perform so much better in regards to high size and complexity of data?

For the most part, NoSQL databases are scalable because they rely on distributed systems and ignore the ACID model. Let's talk through what we gain and what we give up through a distributed system, and then define the ACID model.

When talking about any distributed system (not just storage or databases), there is a concept that defines the limitations of what you can do. This is known as the CAP theorem.

# CAP theorem

*Eric Brewer* introduced the CAP theorem in the year 2000. It states that in any distributed environment, it is impossible for it to provide three guarantees.

- **Consistency**: All the servers in the system will have the same data. So, anyone using the system will get the latest data, regardless of which node they talk to in the distributed system.

- **Availability**: All of the servers will always return data.

- **Partition-tolerance**: The system continues to operate as a whole, even if an individual server fails or cannot be reached.

By looking at these choices, you can tell that it would definitely be ideal to have all three of these things guaranteed, but it's theoretically impossible. In the real world, each NoSQL database picks two of the three options, and usually develops some kind of process to mitigate the impact of the third, unhandled property.

We'll talk about which approach CouchDB takes shortly, but there is still a bit to learn about another concept that NoSQL databases avoid: ACID.

# ACID

**ACID** is a set of properties that apply to database transactions, which are the core of traditional relational databases. While transactions are incredibly powerful, they are also one of the things that make reading and writing quite a bit slower in relational databases.

ACID is made up of four main properties:

- **Atomicity**: This is an all or nothing approach to dealing with data. Everything in the transaction must happen successfully, or none of the changes are committed. This is a key property whenever money or currency is handled in a system, and requires a system of checks and balances.

- **Consistency**: Data will only be accepted if it passes all of the validation in place on the database, such as triggers, data types, and constraints.

- **Isolation**: Transactions will not affect other transactions that are occurring, and other users won't see partial results of a transaction in progress.

- **Durability**: Once the data is saved, it is safe against errors, crashes, and other software malfunctions.

Again, as you read through the definition of ACID, you are probably thinking to yourself, "These are all must haves!" That may be the case, but keep in mind that most NoSQL databases do not fully employ ACID, because it's near impossible to have all of these restrictions and still have blazing fast writes to data.

# So what does all of that mean?

I've given you a lot of definitions now, but let's try to wrap it together into a few simple lists. Let's talk through the advantages and disadvantages of NoSQL databases, when to use, and when to avoid NoSQL databases.

## Advantages of NoSQL databases

With the introduction of NoSQL databases, there are lot of advantages:

- You can do things that simply weren't possible with the processing and query power of traditional relational databases.
- Your data is scalable and flexible, allowing it to scale to size and complexity faster, right out of the box.
- There are new data models to consider. You don't have to force your data into a relational model if it doesn't make sense.
- Writing data is blazing fast.

As you can see, there are some clear advantages of NoSQL databases, but as I mentioned before, there are still some negatives that we need to consider.

## Negatives of NoSQL databases

However, along with the good, there's also some bad:

- There are no common standards; each database does things just a little bit differently
- Querying data does not involve the familiar SQL model to find records
- NoSQL databases are still relatively immature and constantly evolving
- There are new data models to consider; sometimes it can be confusing to make your data fit
- Because a NoSQL database avoids the ACID model, there is no guarantee that all of your data will be successfully written

Some of those negatives may be pretty easy for you to stomach, except for NoSQL's avoidance of the ACID model.

## When you should use NoSQL databases

Now that we have a good take on the advantages and disadvantages, let's talk about some great use cases for using NoSQL databases:

- Applications that have a lot of writing
- Applications where the schema and structure of the data might change

- Large amount of unstructured or semi-structured data
- Traditional relational databases feel restricting, and you want to try something new.

That list isn't exclusive, but there are no clear definitions on when you can use NoSQL databases. Really, you can use them for just about every project.

### When you should avoid NoSQL databases

There are, however, some pretty clear areas that you should avoid when storing data in NoSQL.

- Anything involving money or transactions. What happens if one record doesn't save correctly because of NoSQL avoidance of the ACID model or the data isn't 100 percent available because of the distributed system?
- Business critical data or line of business applications, where missing one row of data could mean huge problems.
- Heavily-structured data requiring functionality in a relational database.

For all of these use cases, you should really focus on using relational databases that will make sure that your data is safe and sound. Of course, you can always include NoSQL databases where it makes sense.

When choosing a database, it's important to remember that "There is no silver bullet." This phrase is used a lot when talking about technology, and it means that there is no one technology that will solve all of your problems without having any side effects or negative consequences. So choose wisely!

# Introduction to CouchDB

For this book and for a variety of my own projects and startups, I chose CouchDB. Let's take a historical look at CouchDB, then quickly touch on its approach to the CAP theorem, and its strengths and weaknesses.

## The history of CouchDB

In April 2005, *Damien Katz* posted a blog entry about a new database engine he was working on, later to be called CouchDB, which is an acronym for **Cluster Of Unreliable Commodity Hardware**. Katz, a former Lotus Notes developer at IBM, was attempting to create a fault-tolerant document database in C++, but soon after, shifted to the **Erlang OTP** platform. As months went by, CouchDB started to evolve under the self-funding of Damien Katz, and in February 2008, it was introduced to the Apache Incubator project. Finally, in November 2008, it graduated as a top-level project.

Damien's team, **CouchOne**, merged with the Membase team in 2011 to form a new company called **Couchbase**. This company was formed to merge **CouchDB** and **Membase** into a new product, and increase the documentation and visibility for the product.

In early 2012, Couchbase announced that it would be shifting focus from facilitating CouchDB and moving to create Couchbase Server 2.0. This new database takes a different approach to the database, which meant that it would not be contributing to the CouchDB community anymore. This news was met with some distress in the CouchDB community until Cloudant stepped in.

**Cloudant**, the chief CouchDB hosting company and creator of BigCouch, a fault tolerant and horizontally scalable clustering frameworking built for CouchDB, announced that they would merge their changes back to CouchDB, and take on the role of continuing development of CouchDB.

In early 2012, at the time of writing, CouchDB's most major release was 1.1.1 in March 31, 2011. But CouchDB 1.2 is looking to be released just around the corner!

# Defining CouchDB

According to `http://couchdb.apache.org/`, CouchDB can be defined as:

◆ A document database server, accessible via a RESTful JSON API

◆ Ad-hoc and schema-free with a flat address space

◆ Distributed, featuring robust, incremental replication with bi-directional conflict detection and management

◆ Query-able and index-able, featuring a table oriented reporting engine that uses JavaScript as a query language.

You might be able to read between the lines, but CouchDB chose availability and partial-tolerance from the CAP theorem, and focuses on eventual consistency using replication.

We could go really deep into what each of these bullet points mean, because it will take the rest of the book until we've touched on them in depth. In each chapter, we'll begin to build on top of our CouchDB knowledge until we have a fully operational application in the wild.

# Summary

I hope you enjoyed this chapter and are ready to take a deep dive into really learning the ins and outs of CouchDB. Let's recap everything we learned in this chapter.

- We talked about the history of databases and the emergence of NoSQL databases
- We defined the advantages and disadvantages of using NoSQL
- We looked at the definition and history of CouchDB

That's it for the history lesson. Fire up your computer. In the next chapter, we'll set everything up to develop web applications with CouchDB and PHP, and make sure that it's all set up correctly.

# 2
# Setting up your Development Environment

*In this chapter, we will set up your computer so that you can develop web applications using PHP and CouchDB. There are a lot of technologies that come into play when developing web applications, so we'll need to make sure that our systems are configured properly before we start writing the code.*

In this chapter, we will:

- ◆ Discuss your operating system and how to install the necessary components
- ◆ Learn about the tools needed to develop PHP and CouchDB applications
- ◆ Configure our web development environment
- ◆ Learn about Homebrew and install CouchDB
- ◆ Use Homebrew to install Git for version control
- ◆ Confirm that you can make a request to CouchDB

Are you ready? Good! Let's get started by talking about operating systems and the role they play in setting up your development environment.

# Operating systems

This book will focus primarily on the Mac OS X Operating System (10.5 and later). While it's possible to develop applications with PHP and CouchDB on any operating system, I will be restricting most of my discussions to Mac OS X for simplicity and brevity. If you're using a Mac, you can skip ahead to the next section, titled *Setting up your web development environment on Mac OS X*.

If you're running Windows or Linux, don't worry! I'll give you some setup tips to get you started, and then you can take it from there. Again, it's worth noting that the command line statements that I use in this book are meant for use on a Mac OS. With that in mind, things such as navigating to your working directory, the location of files, and many more may not work as described.

## Windows

If you're running Windows, there are a few easy steps you need to follow to get your machine up and running.

### Installing Apache and PHP

You can simplify the setup of your Apache and PHP environment by using WAMP (http://www.wampserver.com/en/) or XAMPP (http://www.apachefriends.org/en/xampp.html). Both options make it incredibly easy for you to get Apache and PHP set up with just a few clicks of the mouse.

### Installing Git

**Git** is available for every operating system. To install Git for Windows, navigate to Git's homepage (http://git-scm.com/), and click on the Windows icon.

### Installing CouchDB

You can find more information on installing CouchDB for Windows using Apache's helpful install pages here: http://wiki.apache.org/couchdb/Installing_on_Windows.

## Linux

It's difficult to standardize the install methods for Linux because there are many different flavors and configurations. But if you are using a generic distribution, such as Ubuntu, all of the required tools can be installed with just a few simple command line statements.

# Installing Apache and PHP

`apt-get` is a powerful tool that we'll use to install applications and utilities in your system. Let's start by making sure that `apt-get` is up-to-date, by running the following command:

```
sudo apt-get update
```

Let's make sure that we can host our PHP pages by installing Apache:

```
sudo apt-get install apache2
```

Now that we have Apache, let's install PHP and a few other components needed to run the code in this book:

```
sudo apt-get install php5 php5-dev libapache2-mod-php5 php5-curl php5-mcrypt
```

We have everything that is needed to host websites. So, let's restart Apache in order for our changes to take effect:

```
sudo /etc/init.d/apache2 restart
```

# Installing Git

We'll use Git for source control; luckily installing it is incredibly easy with the help of our friend, `apt-git`. Install Git by running the following command:

```
sudo apt-get install git-core
```

# Installing CouchDB

CouchDB is the database that we'll use through the course of this book. In this section, we'll install and start it using the command line.

1.  Install CouchDB with `apt-get`:

    ```
    sudo apt-get install couchDB
    ```

2.  Start CouchDB as a service by running the following command:

    ```
    sudo /etc/init.d/couchdb start
    ```

That was pretty easy, right? If you are using another Linux distribution, then you might have to do some research on how to get all of the required applications and tools installed.

Now that we got that out of the way, let's discuss the setup of a web development environment for Mac OS X.

# Setting up your web development environment on Mac OS X

In this section, we will go step-by-step and ensure that our development environment is set up correctly. From here on out, I'm assuming you are using a machine that is running Mac OS X without any special modifications to Apache or PHP. If you've done a lot of customization to your development environment, then you probably already know how to configure your machine so that everything works properly.

Now that I've bored you to death with disclaimers, let's get things rolling! The first part of our journey is to meet an application that we will spend a lot of our time with: Terminal.

## Terminal

Terminal is a built-in command line utility for Mac OS X. Using the command line can be a bit of a strange experience when you are just getting started but is extremely powerful once it's mastered. If the basic commands, such as cd, ls, and mkdir look like gibberish to you, then you might want to do some quick research on the UNIX command line.

Here's how you open Terminal:

1. Open **Finder**.
2. Click on **Applications**.
3. Find the folder titled **Utilities**, and open it.
4. Drag the **Terminal** icon right into your dock; you will be using it a lot!
5. Click on the icon for **Terminal** in your dock.

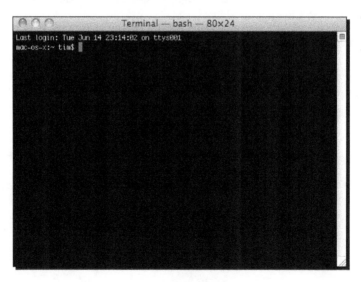

# Time for action – using Terminal to show hidden files

Now that we have `Terminal` up and running, let's get familiar with it by running a quick command that exposes all of the hidden files on your computer. Whether you know it or not, there are a variety of files that are hidden, and they will need to be visible in order for us to complete the setup of our development environment.

1. Start by opening **Terminal**.

2. Type in the following command to allow the Finder to show hidden files, press *Enter* when you are ready:

   ```
   defaults write com.apple.finder AppleShowAllFiles TRUE
   ```

3. In order to see the files, you will need to restart the `Finder`, type the following command, and press *Enter*:

   ```
   killall Finder
   ```

## What just happened?

We just used `Terminal` to run a special command that configured `Finder` to show the hidden files and then ran another command to restart the `Finder`. It's not important for you to remember these commands or fully understand what they mean; you probably will never have to type this again. If you look around your computer you should see quite a few files that you haven't seen before. Here's a quick example of what my hard drive looks like now:

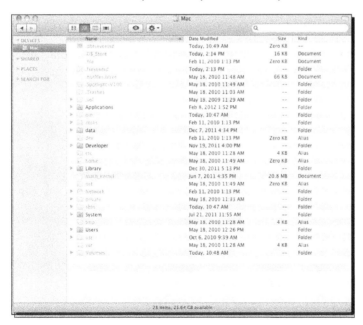

If it irritates you to see so many files, you can hide hidden files again once the setup is complete. You can do this by simply running the following command in `Terminal`: defaults write `com.apple. finder AppleShowAllFiles FALSE`. Then by restarting the `Finder` by running: `killall Finder`.

Now that all of the files on our machine are shown, let's talk about text editors, which will be the primary way you'll view and edit your development project.

# Text editor

In order to write code, you will need a solid text editor. There are a lot of text editors out there, and you can use whichever one you prefer. All of the code in this book will work with any of them. I personally prefer `TextMate` because of its simplicity and ease-of-use.

You can download and install `TextMate` here: `http://macromates.com/`.

# Apache

**Apache** is an open source web server and the engine that will run the PHP code that you'll write in this book. Luckily, Apache comes pre-installed on all installations of Mac OS X, so all we need to do is start it using `Terminal`.

1. Open **Terminal**.

2. Run the following command to start Apache:

   ```
   sudo apachectl start
   ```

That's all it takes to get Apache up and running on your computer. Apache won't let you turn it on if it's already running. Try typing that same statement again; your machine will alert you that it's already running:

```
● ○ ○        tim@mac-os-x:~ — bash — 61×10
tim:~ $ sudo apachectl start
tim:~ $ sudo apachectl start
org.apache.httpd: Already loaded
tim:~ $ █
```

It's very unlikely, but on the off chance that your machine does not have Apache installed, you can install it by following the instructions on Apache's website: `http://httpd.apache.org/docs/2.0/install.html`.

# Web browser

You probably use a web browser every day when surfing the Internet, but it will also double up as a powerful debugging tool for us. I will use Chrome as my web browser, but the up-to-date versions of Safari, Firefox, or Internet Explorer will work just fine as well. Let's use our web browser to check that Apache is accessible.

## Time for action – opening your web browser

We are going to access the Apache service on our machine by opening a web browser, and navigating to Apache's URL.

1.  Open your web browser.

2.  Type `http://localhost` into the address bar, and hit *Enter*.

3.  Your browser will display the following message to you:

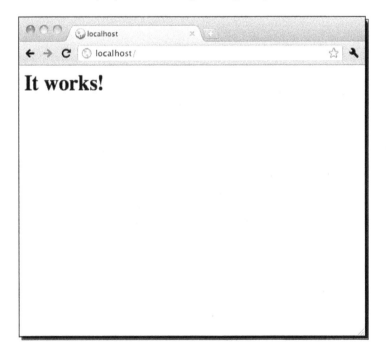

## *What just happened?*

We used the web browser to access Apache, and in return, it showed us a quick verification that everything was hooked up correctly. Our computer knew that we were trying to access our local Apache service because of the URL `http://localhost`. The URL `http://localhost` actually maps to the address `http://127.0.0.1:80`, which is the address and port of the Apache service. You will see `127.0.0.1` come up again when we discuss CouchDB.

## PHP

`PHP` is in the title of this book, so you know it will play a big part in the development process. PHP is already installed on your machine, so you have nothing to install. Let's just double check that you can access PHP by using Terminal.

## Time for action – checking your PHP version

We are going to check that PHP is working on your computer by accessing it with Terminal.

1. Open **Terminal**.

2. Run the following command for PHP to return its version:

   ```
   php -v
   ```

3. **Terminal** will respond with something similar to the following:

```
mac-os-x:~ tim$ php -v
PHP 5.3.4 (cli) (built: Dec 15 2010 12:15:07)
Copyright (c) 1997-2010 The PHP Group
Zend Engine v2.3.0, Copyright (c) 1998-2010 Zend Technologies
mac-os-x:~ tim$
```

## *What just happened?*

We used **Terminal** to ensure that we had PHP running correctly on our machine. Not only did we check to make sure that PHP was accessible, but we also asked for its version. Your version may differ slightly from mine, but it only matters that your version is PHP 5.3 or higher.

If your version is lower than PHP 5.3 or you were unable to get PHP to respond, you can install or upgrade by looking at PHP's manual: `http://php.net/manual/en/install.macosx.php`.

## Time for action – making sure that Apache can connect to PHP

In order to create a web application, Apache needs to be able to run the PHP code. So, we are going to check that Apache can access PHP.

*1.* Use **Finder** to navigate to the following folder: `/etc/apache2`.

*2.* Open the file named `httpd.conf` in your text editor.

*3.* Look through the file, and find the following line (it should be around line `116`):

```
#LoadModule php5_module libexec/apache2/libphp5.so
```

*4.* Remove the hash (#) symbol that is in front of this string to uncomment this line of the `config` file. It's possible that your configuration file may already have this uncommented. If it does, then you don't have to change anything. Regardless, the end result should look as follows:

```
LoadModule php5_module libexec/apache2/libphp5.so
```

*5.* Open **Terminal**.

*6.* Restart Apache by running the following command:

```
sudo apachectl restart
```

### What just happened?

We opened Apache's main configuration file, `httpd.conf`, and uncommented a line so that Apache can load PHP. We then restarted the Apache server, so that the updated configuration would take effect.

## Time for action – creating a quick info page

We are going to double-check that Apache can render PHP scripts by quickly creating a `phpinfo` page that will display a wide array of data about your configuration.

*1.* Open your text editor.

**2.** Create a new file that contains the following code:

```
<?php phpinfo(); ?>
```

**3.** Save the file with the name, `info.php`, and save that file in the following location: `/Library/WebServer/Documents/info.php`.

**4.** Open your browser.

**5.** Navigate your browser to `http://localhost/info.php`.

**6.** Your browser will display the following page:

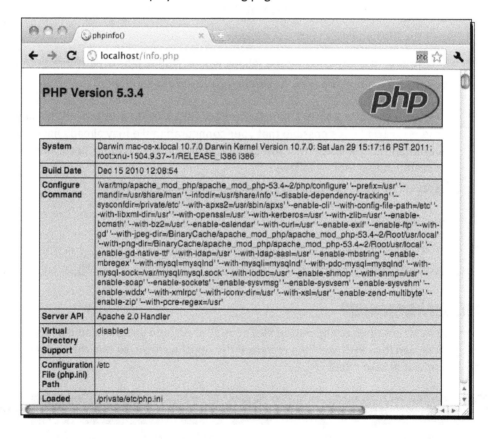

## What just happened?

We used our text editor to create a file called `info.php` that contained a special PHP function called `phpinfo`. We saved the `info.php` file into the folder: `/Library/Webserver/Documents`. This folder is the default location (in Mac OS X only) for all of the files that your Apache service will display. When your browser hit the `info.php` page, the `phpinfo` looked at your PHP installation and returned an HTML file with details about your configuration. You can tell that there is a lot going on here. Feel free to poke around and look at some of the information before we move on.

## Fine tuning Apache

We finally have our basic web development environment set up. However there are a few things we'll need to adjust in Apache in order for us to build our application; the first of which is enabling a great built-in module called `mod_rewrite`.

## Time for action – further configuration of Apache

`mod_rewrite` will allow us to rewrite the requested URLs on the fly, which will help us build an application with clean URLs. The rewriting itself is handled in another Apache configuration file called `.htaccess`, which we will touch on in *Chapter 4, Starting Your Application*. In the following section, we'll configure Apache, so that `mod_rewrite` is enabled.

1. Use **Finder** to navigate to the following folder: `/etc/apache2`.

2. Locate and open a file named `httpd.conf` in your text editor.

3. Look through the file, and find this line (it should be line `114`):

   `#LoadModule rewrite_module libexec/apache2/mod_rewrite.so`

4. Uncomment the line by removing the hash (#) symbol. It's possible that your system is already configured to enable `mod_rewrite`. Regardless, make sure it matches the following code:

   `LoadModule rewrite_module libexec/apache2/mod_rewrite.so`

5. Look through the file, and find this chunk of code (it should go from line `178-183`):

   ```
   <Directory />
     Options FollowSymLinks
     AllowOverride None
     Order deny,allow
     Allow from all
   </Directory>
   ```

6. Alter the line of code that says `AllowOverride None` and change it to say
`AllowOverride All`. The resulting section should look as follows:

```
<Directory />
  Options FollowSymLinks
  AllowOverride All
  Order deny,allow
  Allow from all
</Directory>
```

7. Keep scrolling through the file until you find this chunk of code (should go from line
210-215):

```
#
# AllowOverride controls what directives may be placed in
#.htaccess files.
# It can be "All", "None", or any combination of the keywords:
#    Options FileInfo AuthConfig Limit
#
AllowOverride None
```

8. Alter the line of this code that says `AllowOverride None` and change it to read
`AllowOverride All`. The resulting section should look as follows:

```
#
# AllowOverride controls what directives may be placed in
#.htaccess files.
# It can be "All", "None", or any combination of the keywords:
#    Options FileInfo AuthConfig Limit
#
AllowOverride All
```

9. Open **Terminal**.

10. Restart Apache by running the following command:

```
sudo apachectl restart
```

## What just happened?

We just configured Apache so that it can operate more freely and include the ability to
rewrite URLs using the `mod_rewrite` module. We then changed the configuration of
`AllowOverride` from `None` to `All`. `AllowOverride` tells the server what to do when
it finds the `.htaccess` file. With this being set to `None`, the `.htaccess` file is ignored.
Changing the setting to `All` allows settings to be overridden in an `.htaccess` file. This is
exactly what we'll do as we start building out our application in *Chapter 4*.

# Our web development setup is complete!

We now have everything set up for us to create standard web applications. We have Apache handling requests. We have PHP connected and responding to calls from Apache, and we have our text editor ready for any code that we can throw at it.

There are still a few pieces missing for us to have a complete development environment. In the next section, we will install CouchDB as our database.

# Installing CouchDB

In this section, we will install CouchDB 1.0 onto your machine and get it prepared for development. There are a variety of ways to get CouchDB on your machine, so if you have issues with the following install process, please reference CouchDB's website here: `http://wiki.apache.org/couchdb/Installation`.

# Homebrew

In order to install the rest of the components that we will use in this book, we will use a utility called **Homebrew**. Homebrew is the easiest way to install the UNIX tools that Apple left out of OSX. Before we can use Homebrew to install other tools, we first need to install Homebrew.

## Time for action – installing Homebrew

We are going to use **Terminal** to download Homebrew and install it onto our computer.

1. Open **Terminal**.

2. Type the following commands into **Terminal**, pressing *Enter* after each line:

   ```
   sudo mkdir -p /usr/local
   sudo chown -R $USER /usr/local
   curl -Lf http://github.com/mxcl/homebrew/tarball/master | tar xz
   -- strip 1 -C/usr/local
   ```

3. **Terminal** will respond with a progress bar and show you how the installation process went. When the installation is complete, you will receive a success message, and you will have control of the **Terminal** again.

## What just happened?

We added the directory /usr/local, which is where Homebrew will save all of its files. Then we made sure that the folder was owned by us (the current user). We then installed Homebrew using a cURL statement to grab the repository from Github (I'll cover cURL later in this chapter; we are going to use it quite a bit). After grabbing the repository, it was unzipped, using the command line function tar, and placed into the /usr/local folder.

## Time for action – installing CouchDB

Now that we have Homebrew installed, we are finally ready to install CouchDB.

 Please note that before Homebrew installs CouchDB, it will install all of its dependencies, which include such things as: Erlang, Spidermonkey, ICU, and so on. This section might take up to 10-15 minutes to complete, because they are being compiled locally on your machine. Don't worry if it seems like it's taking too long; this is normal.

We are going to install CouchDB using Homebrew.

1. Open Terminal

2. Run the following command:

   ```
   brew install couchdb -v
   ```

3. Terminal will respond with a lot of text over the next couple of minutes. You will see it grab each dependency and then install it. At the very end, you will receive a success message.

## What just happened?

We just installed CouchDB from the source and downloaded all of its dependencies. After installation, Homebrew put everything in the right folders and configured everything we need to use CouchDB.

# Checking that our setup is complete

We just accomplished a lot in the past few pages. We've set up our web development environment and installed CouchDB. Now, let's double check that we can run and access CouchDB.

# Starting CouchDB

CouchDB is easy to manage. It operates as a service that we can start and stop by using our command line. Let's start CouchDB with a command line statement.

1. Open **Terminal**.

2. Run the following command:

   ```
   couchdb -b
   ```

3. **Terminal** will reply with the following:

   ```
   Apache CouchDB has started, time to relax.
   ```

Great! Now that we have started CouchDB as a background process, it will sit in the background and handle requests until we shut it off.

## Time for action – checking that CouchDB is running

We are going to attempt to hit the CouchDB service on our machine by using the command line utility cURL (we'll spell it curl from here on out for the sake of simplicity) that allows you to make raw HTTP requests. curl is our main method of communication with CouchDB. Let's start with a curl statement to talk to CouchDB.

1. Open **Terminal**.

2. Run the following statement to create a request that will hit CouchDB:

   ```
   curl http://127.0.0.1:5984/
   ```

3. **Terminal** will reply with the following:

   ```
   {"couchdb":"Welcome","version":"1.0.2"}
   ```

## *What just happened?*

We just used curl to communicate with the CouchDB service by issuing a GET request. By default, curl will assume that we're trying to issue a GET request unless we tell it otherwise. We issued our curl statement to http://127.0.0.1:5984. Breaking this resource down into pieces, http://127.0.0.1 is the IP of our local computer, and 5984 is the port that CouchDB runs on by default.

# Running CouchDB as a background process

If we were to stop our configuration here, you would have to run `couchdb -b` each time you started development. This will quickly turn into a pain point for us. So, let's run CouchDB as a system daemon that will always run in the background, even after you restart your computer. In order to do this, we will use a Mac OS X service management framework, called `launchd`, that manages system daemons and allows them to be started and stopped.

1. Open **Terminal**.

2. Kill the background process of CouchDB, by running the following command:

   ```
   couchdb -k
   ```

3. If CouchDB was running, it would return the following text:

   ```
   Apache CouchDB has been killed.
   ```

4. Let's run CouchDB as a real background process and ensure that it starts each time you start your computer by running the following statement:

   ```
   launchctl load -w /usr/local/Cellar/couchdb/1.0.2/Library/
   LaunchDaemons/org.apache.couchdb.plist
   ```

 If your version of CouchDB is different to mine, you will have to change the version in this script that says "1.0.2", to match your version.

CouchDB is now running in the background, and even if we restart our computer, we don't have to worry about starting the service before we try to use it.

If, for some reason, you decide that you don't want CouchDB running in the background, you can unload it by running the following command:

```
launchctl unload /usr/local/Cellar/couchdb/1.0.2/Library/LaunchDaemons/
org.apache.couchdb.plist
```

You can double-check to make sure that CouchDB is running by using the `curl` statement that we used earlier:

1. Open **Terminal**.

2. Run the following command:

   ```
   curl http://127.0.0.1:5984/
   ```

3. **Terminal** will reply with the following:

   ```
   {"couchdb":"Welcome","version":"1.0.2"}
   ```

# Installing version control

Version control systems allow developers to track code changes, merge other developers' code, and to roll back any inadvertent errors. Version control systems are a must on a project with several developers but can also be a lifesaver for single developer projects. Think of it as a safety net—if you accidentally do something you didn't want to, then source control is there to protect you. There are several options when it comes to version control, but in this book, we will use Git.

## Git

Git (`http://git-scm.com/`) has become one of the more popular and widely adopted version control systems because of its distributed nature and ease-of-use. The only thing easier than actually using Git is installing it. We will use Homebrew to install Git, just as we did with CouchDB.

## Time for action – installing and configuring Git

Get ready! We are going to install Git onto our computer using Homebrew.

1.  Open **Terminal**.

2.  Run the following command to install Git using Homebrew:

    ```
    brew install git
    ```

3.  **Terminal** will download and install Git for you in just a matter of moments. It will then respond with a success message telling you that Git has been installed.

4.  After Git has been installed, you need to configure it so that it knows who you are when you commit changes to data. Run the following commands to identify yourself and make sure to fill in your own information where I've put Your Name and your_email@domain.com:

    ```
    git config -global user.name "Your Name"
    git config -global user.email your_email@domain.com
    ```

## What just happened?

We just installed Git from the source using Homebrew. We then configured Git to use our name and e-mail address. These settings will make sure that any changes that are committed to source control from this machine are identified.

# Did you have any problems?

We're all done with configuring our system! In a perfect world, everything would be installed without any issues, but it's entirely possible that something didn't install perfectly. If it seems like something isn't working right, or you think you may have made some typos along the way, I have a script that you can run that will help you get back on track. This command can be executed locally by calling a file I have on github. All you have to do is run the following command in **Terminal**, and it will run all of the necessary code for this chapter:

```
sh <(curl -s https://raw.github.com/timjuravich/environment-setup/master/
configure.sh)
```

This script will do all of the work that has been mentioned in this section, and it's safe to run as many times as you want. I could have given you this one command and finished up the chapter pages ago, but this chapter was integral in teaching you how to use the tools and utilities that we will use in the coming chapters.

## Pop quiz

1. When we are using the default Apache installation for web developing, where is the default working directory?

2. In order to use our local development environment with CouchDB, we need to make sure that two services are running. What are they, and how do you make them run in **Terminal**?

3. What command line statement do you use to issue a Get request to CouchDB?

# Summary

Let's do a quick recap of everything we've covered in this chapter:

◆ We became familiar with **Terminal** and used it to show hidden files

◆ We installed a text editor for us to use in development

◆ We learned how to configure Apache and how to interact with it through the command line

◆ We learned how to create simple PHP files and placed them in the correct location so that Apache could display them

◆ We learned how to install Homebrew, and then we used it to install CouchDB and Git

◆ We checked to make sure that CouchDB was up and running

In the next chapter, we'll get more familiar with CouchDB and explore how to use it in the creation of our web application.

# 3
# Getting Started with CouchDB and Futon

*In the previous chapter, we set up our development environment, and I'm sure that you are chomping at the bit to find out what CouchDB can do for us. On that note, we're going to spend this entire chapter digging into CouchDB.*

Specifically, we will:

◆ Dive into what CouchDB means and learn how it looks in the databases and documents

◆ Learn how we'll interact with CouchDB through its RESTful JSON API

◆ Use CouchDB's built in administrative console: Futon

◆ Learn how to add security to your CouchDB databases

## What is CouchDB?

The first sentence of CouchDB's definition (as defined by `http://couchdb.apache.org/`) is as follows:

> *CouchDB is a document database server, accessible through the RESTful JSON API.*

Let's dissect this sentence to fully understand what it means. Let's start with the term **database server**.

# Database server

CouchDB employs a document-oriented database management system that serves a flat collection of documents with no schema, grouping, or hierarchy. This is a concept that **NoSQL** has introduced, and is a big departure from relational databases (such as MySQL), where you would expect to see tables, relationships, and foreign keys. Every developer has experienced a project where they have had to force a relational database schema into a project that really didn't require the rigidity of tables and complex relationships. This is where CouchDB does things differently; it stores all of the data in a self-contained object with no set schema. The following diagram will help to illustrate this:

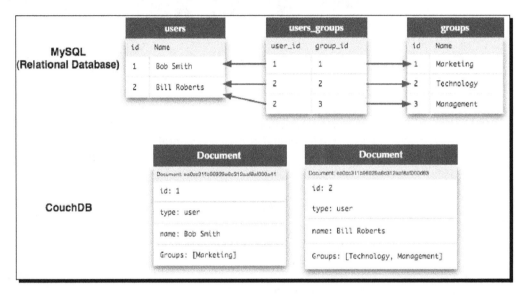

In the previous example, we might want to facilitate the ability for many users to belong to one-to-many groups. In order to handle this functionality in a relational database (such as MySQL), we would create a users table, a groups table, and a link table, called users_groups, that allow you to map many users to many groups. This practice is common to most web applications.

Now look at the CouchDB documents. There are no tables or link tables, just documents. These documents contain all of the data pertaining to a single object.

> This diagram is very simplified. If we wanted to create more logic around the groups in CouchDB, we would have had to create **group** documents, with a simple relationship between the user documents and group documents. We'll touch on how to handle this type of relationship as we get deeper into the book.

We saw the term **document** quite a bit in this section. So let's dig further into what documents are and how CouchDB uses them.

# Documents

To illustrate how you might use documents, first imagine that you are physically filling out the paper form of a job application. This form has information about you, your address, and past addresses. It also has information about many of your past jobs, education, certifications, and much more. A document would save all of this data exactly in the way you would see it in the physical form - all in one place, without any unnecessary complexity.

In CouchDB, documents are stored as JSON objects that contain key and value pairs. Each document has reserved fields for metadata such as id, revision, and deleted. Besides the reserved fields, documents are 100 percent schema-less, meaning that each document can be formatted and treated independently with as many different variations as you might need.

## Example of a CouchDB document

Let's take a look at an example of what a CouchDB document might look like for a blog post:

```
{
    "_id": "431f956fa44b3629ba924eab05000553",
    "_rev": "1-c46916a8efe63fb8fec6d097007bd1c6",
    "title": "Why I like Chicken",
    "author": "Tim Juravich",
    "tags": [
        "Chicken",
        "Grilled",
        "Tasty"
    ],
    "body": "I like chicken, especially when it's grilled."
}
```

## JSON format

The first thing you might notice is the strange markup of the document, which is **JavaScript Object Notation (JSON)**. JSON is a lightweight data-interchange format based on JavaScript syntax and is extremely portable. CouchDB uses JSON for all communication with it, so you'll get very familiar with it through the course of this book.

## Key-value storage

The next thing that you might notice is that there is a lot of information in this document. There are key-value pairs that are simple to understand, such as `"title"`, `"author"`, and `"body"`, but you'll also notice that `"tags"` is an array of strings. CouchDB lets you embed as much information as you want directly into a document. This is a concept that might be new to relational database users who are used to normalized and structured databases.

## Reserved fields

We mentioned reserved fields earlier on. Let's look at the two reserved fields that you saw in the previous example document: `_id` and `_rev`.

`_id` is the unique identifier of the document. This means that `_id` is mandatory, and no two documents can have the same value. If you don't define an `_id` on creation of a document, CouchDB will choose a unique one for you.

`_rev` is the revision version of the document and is the field that helps drive CouchDB's version control system. Each time you save a document, the revision number is required so that CouchDB knows which version of the document is the newest. This is required because CouchDB does not use a locking mechanism, meaning that if two people are updating a document at the same time, then the first one to save his/her changes first, wins. One of the unique things about CouchDB's revision system is that each time a document is saved, the original document is not overwritten, and a new document is created with the new data, while CouchDB stores a backup of the previous documents in its original form in an archive. Old revisions remain available until the database is compacted, or some cleanup action occurs.

The last piece of the definition sentence is the RESTful JSON API. So, let's cover that next.

# RESTful JSON API

In order to understand REST, let's first define **HyperText Transfer Protocol** (**HTTP**). HTTP is the underlying protocol of the Internet that defines how messages are formatted and transmitted and how services should respond when using a variety of methods. These methods consist of four main verbs, such as GET, PUT, POST, and DELETE. In order to fully understand how HTTP methods function, let's first define REST.

**Representation State Transfer** (**REST**) is a stateless protocol that accesses addressable resources through HTTP methods. **Stateless** means that each request contains all of the information necessary to completely understand and use the data in the request, and **addressable resources** means that you can access the object via a URL.

That might not mean a lot in itself, but, by putting all of these ideas together, it becomes a powerful concept. Let's illustrate the power of REST by looking at two examples:

| Resource | GET | PUT | POST | DELETE |
|---|---|---|---|---|
| `http://localhost/collection` | **Read** a list of all of the items inside of `collection` | **Update** the `collection` with another `collection` | **Create** a new `collection` | **Delete** the `collection` |
| `http://localhost/collection/abc123` | **Read** the details of the `abc123` item inside of `collection` | **Update** the details of `abc123` inside of `collection` | **Create** a new object `abc123` inside of a `collection` | **Delete** `abc123` from `collection` |

By looking at the table, you can see that each resource is in the form of a URL. The first resource is `collection`, and the second resource is `abc123`, which lives inside of `collection`. Each of these resources responds differently when you pass different methods to them. This is the beauty of REST and HTTP working together.

Notice the bold words I used in the table: **Read**, **Update**, **Create**, and **Delete**. These words are actually, in themselves, another concept, and it, of course, has its own term; **CRUD**. The unflattering term CRUD stands for Create, Read, Update, and Delete and is a concept that REST uses to define what happens to a defined resource when an HTTP method is combined with a resource in the form of a URL. So, if you were to boil all of this down, you would come to the following diagram:

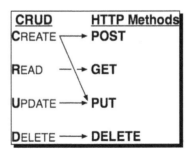

This diagram means:

- In order to **CREATE** a resource, you can use either the **POST** or **PUT** method
- In order **READ** a resource, you need to use the **GET** method
- In order to **UPDATE** a resource, you need to use the **PUT** method
- In order to **DELETE** a resource, you need to use the **DELETE** method

As you can see, this concept of CRUD makes it really clear to find out what method you need to use when you want to perform a specific action.

Now that we've looked at what REST means, let's move onto the term **API**, which means **Application Programming Interface**. While there are a lot of different use cases and concepts of APIs, an API is what we'll use to programmatically interact with CouchDB.

Now that we have defined all of the terms, the RESTful JSON API could be defined as follows: we have the ability to interact with CouchDB by issuing an HTTP request to the CouchDB API with a defined resource, HTTP method, and any additional data. Combining all of these things means that we are using REST. After CouchDB processes our REST request, it will return with a JSON-formatted response with the result of the request.

All of this background knowledge will start to make sense as we play with CouchDB's RESTful JSON API, by going through each of the HTTP methods, one at a time.

We will use curl (which we learned to use in the previous chapter) to explore each of the HTTP methods by issuing raw HTTP requests.

## Time for action – getting a list of all databases in CouchDB

You've seen a GET request earlier in this book when we used the curl statement:
curl http://localhost:5984.

This time, let's issue a GET request to access CouchDB and get a list of all of the databases on the server.

1. Run the following command in **Terminal**:
   ```
   curl -X GET http://localhost:5984/_all_dbs
   ```

2. **Terminal** will respond with the following:
   ```
   ["_users"]
   ```

## What just happened?

We used **Terminal** to trigger a GET request to CouchDB's RESTful JSON API. We used one of the options: -X, of curl, to define the HTTP method. In this instance, we used GET. GET is the default method, so technically you could omit -X if you wanted to. Once CouchDB processes the request, it sends back a list of the databases that are in the CouchDB server. Currently, there is only the _users database, which is a default database that CouchDB uses to authenticate users.

# Time for action – creating new databases in CouchDB

In this exercise, we'll issue a `PUT` request, which will create a new database in CouchDB.

1. Create a new database by running the following command in **Terminal**:

   ```
   curl -X PUT http://localhost:5984/test-db
   ```

2. **Terminal** will respond with the following:

   ```
   {"ok":true}
   ```

3. Try creating another database with the same name by running the following command in **Terminal**:

   ```
   curl -X PUT http://localhost:5984/test-db
   ```

4. **Terminal** will respond with the following:

   ```
   {"error":"file_exists","reason":"The database could not be
   created, the file already exists."}
   ```

5. Okay, that didn't work. So let's to try to create a database with a different name by running the following command in **Terminal**:

   ```
   curl -X PUT http://localhost:5984/another-db
   ```

6. **Terminal** will respond with the following:

   ```
   {"ok":true}
   ```

7. Let's check the details of the `test-db` database quickly and see more detailed information about it. To do that, run the following command in **Terminal**:

   ```
   curl -X GET http://localhost:5984/test-db
   ```

8. **Terminal** will respond with something similar to this (I re-formatted mine for readability):

   ```
   {
       "committed_update_seq": 1,
       "compact_running": false,
       "db_name": "test-db",
       "disk_format_version": 5,
       "disk_size": 4182,
       "doc_count": 0,
       "doc_del_count": 0,
   ```

```
        "instance_start_time": "1308863484343052",
        "purge_seq": 0,
        "update_seq": 1
}
```

## What just happened?

We just used **Terminal** to trigger a PUT method to the created databases through CouchDB's RESTful JSON API, by passing test-db as the name of the database that we wanted to create at the end of the CouchDB root URL. When the database was successfully created, we received a message that everything went okay.

Next, we created a PUT request to create another database with the same name test-db. Because there can't be more than one database with the same name, we received an error message.

We then used a PUT request to create a new database again, named another-db. When the database was successfully created, we received a message that everything went okay.

Finally, we issued a GET request to our test-db database to find out more information on the database. It's not important to know exactly what each of these statistics mean, but it's a useful way to get an overview of a database.

It's worth noting that the URL that was called in the final GET request was the same URL we called when we first created the database. The only difference is that we changed the HTTP method from PUT to GET. This is REST in action!

## Time for action – deleting a database In CouchDB

In this exercise, we'll call a DELETE request to delete the another-db database.

1. Delete another-db by running the following command in **Terminal**:

    ```
    curl -X DELETE http://localhost:5984/another-db
    ```

2. **Terminal** will respond with the following:

    ```
    {"ok":true}
    ```

## What just happened?

We used **Terminal** to trigger a DELETE method to CouchDB's RESTful JSON API. We passed the name of the database that we wanted to delete, another-db, at the end of the root URL. When the database was successfully deleted, we received a message that everything went okay.

## Time for action – creating a CouchDB document

In this exercise, we'll create a document by initiating a POST call. You'll notice that our curl statement will start to get a bit more complex.

**1.** Create a document in the test-db database by running the following command in **Terminal**:

```
curl -X POST -H "Content-Type:application/json" -d '{"type":
"customer", "name":"Tim Juravich", "location":"Seattle, WA"}'
http://localhost:5984/test-db
```

**2.** **Terminal** will respond with something similar to the following:

```
{"ok":true,"id":"39b1fe3cdcc7e7006694df91fb002082","rev":"1-8cf37e
845c61cc239f0e98f8b7f56311"}
```

**3.** Let's retrieve the newly created document from CouchDB. Start by copying the ID you were returned at the last response of the **Terminal** to your clipboard; mine is 39b1fe3cdcc7e7006694df91fb002082, but yours will be different. Then run this command in **Terminal**, pasting your ID at the end of the URL:

```
curl -X GET http://localhost:5984/test-db/41198fc6e20d867525a8faeb
7a000015 | python -mjson.tool
```

**4.** **Terminal** will respond with something similar to the following:

```
{
    "_id": "41198fc6e20d867525a8faeb7a000015",
    "_rev": "1-4cee6ca6966fcf1f8ea7980ba3b1805e",
    "location": "Seattle, WA",
    "name": "Tim Juravich",
    "type:": "customer"
}
```

## What just happened?

We used **Terminal** to trigger a POST call to CouchDB's RESTful JSON API. This time, our curl statement gained some more options that we haven't used before. The -H option enables us to set the header of the HTTP request for POST methods. We need to set the content-type to JSON so that CouchDB's RESTful API knows what format is coming in. We also used a new option, -d option, which stands for data. The data option allows us to pass data in the form of a string along with our curl statement.

After creating our document, we retrieved it to **Terminal** by submitting a GET request to `http://localhost:5984/test-db/41198fc6e20d867525a8faeb7a000015`. In response, we received a JSON object containing all of the document's data. At the end of this request, we did something a little different. We added `python —mjson.tool`, which is a built-in component from Python that enables us to nicely format our JSON responses, so that we can make more sense of them. This will come in handy as we start looking at more complex documents.

 I didn't mention that you needed Python installed earlier in the book because this is a *nice to have* feature. If you receive an error because you are missing Python, you can either install it by going here: `http://python.org/download/`.

I know that this has been a bit tiresome, but `curl` will be the main method that our PHP code will use to talk to CouchDB, so it's important that we're familiar with how it works. Luckily, there is an easier way to access and manage your data through a tool named **Futon**.

# Futon

CouchDB comes with a built-in web-based administration console called Futon. Futon allows you to manage databases, users, and documents in a simple interface. The best part of Futon is that it's already installed and ready to go, since it comes packed with CouchDB.

Let's check it out:

1. Open your browser.

2. Go to `http://localhost:5984/_utils/`.

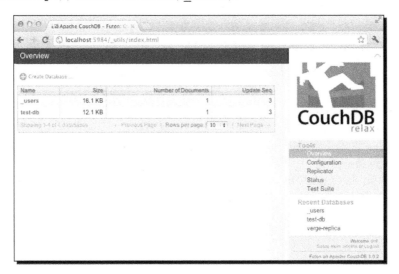

This is Futon's **Overview** page. On this page, you can see all of the databases in the CouchDB installation and the ability to create new ones. You should see the database `test-db` that we created in the previous steps, and you can also see the `_users` database that is in the CouchDB installation by default.

If you look to the right-side of the window, you'll see **Tools**. We will use this when we cover *Replicator* later in the book.

**3.** Let's dig further into our database `test-db` by clicking on the link for `test-db` in the database list on the **Overview** page.

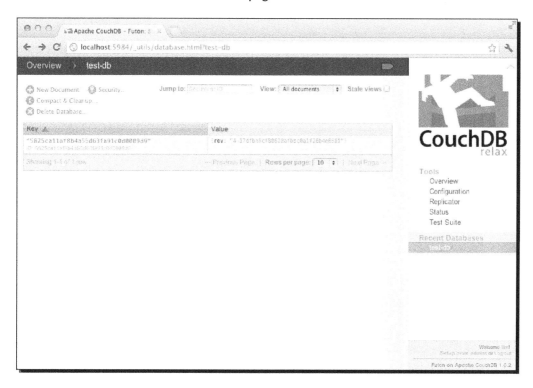

The page you see is the database detail. In this page, you can see a list of all of the documents that are in our database along with some actions that you can perform on the selected database such as **New Document**, **Security**, **Compact & Cleanup...**, **Delete Database**, **Search**, and so on. It's worth noting that Futon is just a helper, and all of these functions are available through `curl` as well.

**4.** Let's dig deeper into Futon by clicking on on a document, and you'll be forwarded to the document detail.

This data should look familiar! All of our keys are listed on the left, and the values are listed on the right.

## Time for action – updating a document in Futon

Using Futon, you can easily update the values of this document. Let's go through a quick example.

**1.** Make sure you have the document open in your browser.

**2.** Note the value of _rev in your document.

**3.** Double-click the value of the **location** field: **Seattle**, **WA**, and change it to **New York**, **NY**.

**4.** Click on **Save Document** at the top of the page.

**5.** Check to make sure that the value of _rev in your document has changed, and that **New York**, **NY** is now the value of location.

## *What just happened?*

You just used Futon to change the value of a field in our document and then saved changes to update the document. When the document refreshed, you should have noticed that the `_rev` field has changed, and your change to the field was updated.

You may have also noticed that **Previous Version** looks like it's clickable now. Click on it and see what happens. Futon displays the old version of the document with **Seattle**, **WA** in the location, as opposed to the new value of **New York**, **NY**.

You will now see CouchDB's revisions in full effect. If you want to, you can cycle through all of the versions of the document using the **Previous Version** and **Next Version** links.

There are two important things we need to note about CouchDB's revision system:

You cannot update an old version of a document; if you try to save an old version of a document, CouchDB will return a document update conflict error. This is because the only real version of the document is the most current one.

Your revision history is only temporary. If your database kept a record of every single change, it would start to really get bloated. So, CouchDB has a feature called **Compaction** that will get rid of any of the old revisions.

## Time for action – creating a document in Futon

We've gone through the updating of existing documents. Let's create a document from scratch in Futon.

1.  Go to the database overview by clicking on the database name, `test-db`, in the header.

2.  Click on **New Document**.

3.  A blank document is created and ready for us to put in new fields. Notice that the `_id` is already set for us (but we can change it if we want).

4.  Click on **Add Field** to create a new field, and call it `location`.

5.  Double-click on the value right next to the label that says **null**, and enter in your current location.

6.  Click on **Add Field** to create a new field, and call it `name`.

7.  Double-click on the value right next to the label that says `null`, and enter in your name.

**8.** Click on **Save Document** at the top of the page.

**9.** The document has been saved. Notice that it now has a `_rev` value set.

## What just happened?

You just used Futon to create a document from scratch. When the document was first created, CouchDB created a unique ID for you to set it as the value of the `_id` field. Next, you added the `name` field and inputted your name as its value. Finally, you saved it to create a new document. We've talked about how documents can have completely different fields, but this is the first time we've actually done it!

# Security

Up to this point, we've created, read, updated, and deleted documents and databases, and we've done all of this without any type of security. When you don't have any administrators on your CouchDB instance, it's called **Admin Party**, and that simply means that CouchDB will process any request from anybody for anything.

## Time for action – taking CouchDB out of Admin Party

Having CouchDB unsecure isn't bad when you are programming locally, but it can be catastrophic if you accidentally have an unsecure database on a publicly accessible server. Let's briefly add security now to make sure you know how to do it in the future.

**1.** Open Futon to the **Overview**, and look at the bottom right corner. You'll see text that says:

```
Welcome to Admin Party!
Everyone is admin. Fix this.
```

**2.** Click on the **Fix this** link.

**3.** A new window will pop up, prompting you **Create Server Admin**.

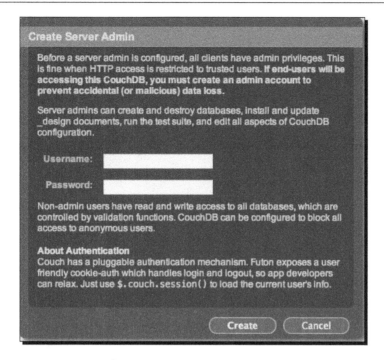

4. Enter in a username and password that you want to use for your administrator account, and click on **Create**.

## *What just happened?*

You just used Futon to add a server admin to your CouchDB installation. The **Create Server Admin** pop up said that once a server admin was added, you would be able to create and destroy databases, and perform other administrative functions. All other users (including anonymous users) can still read and write to the databases. With that in mind, we'll want to add some security onto the database as well.

## Time for action – anonymously accessing the _users database

Let's go through a quick exercise of calling a `curl` statement to the _users database to see why it's important to secure our data.

1. Open **Terminal**.

2. Run the following command, replacing `your_username` with the username of the server admin that you just created.

```
curl localhost:5984/_users/org.couchdb.user:your_username | python
-mjson.tool
```

**3.** **Terminal** will respond with something similar to:

```
{
    "_id": "org.couchdb.user:your_username",
    "_rev": "1-b9af54a7cdc392c2c298591f0dcd81f3",
    "name": "your_username",
    "password_sha": "3bc7d6d86da61fed6d4d82e1e4d1c3ca587aecc8",
    "roles": [],
    "salt": "9812acc4866acdec35c903f0cc072c1d",
    "type": "user"
}
```

## What just happened?

You used **Terminal** to create a `curl` request to read the document containing your server admin's data. The passwords in the database are encrypted, but it's possible that someone could still unencrypt the password or use the usernames of the users against them. With that in mind, let's secure the database so that only administrators can access this database.

## Time for action – securing the _users database

Let's secure the _users database so that only server admins can read, write, and edit the other users within the system.

**1.** Open Futon to the **Overview**.

**2.** Click on the _users database.

**3.** Click on **Security** at the top of the screen.

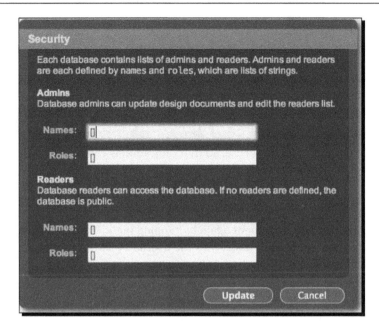

**4.** Change the values of **Roles** for both **Admins** and **Readers** to `["admins"]`, so it looks as follows:

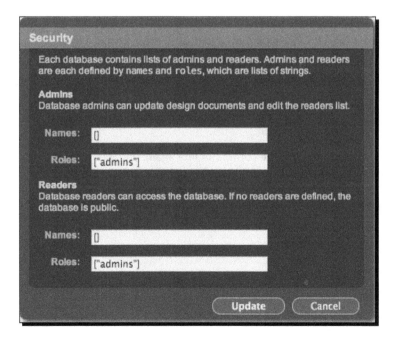

## What just happened?

You just changed the roles of **Admins** and **Readers** for the _users database to ["admins"], so that only admins could read or alter the design documents and readers' list. We made the format of the roles ["admins"] because it accepts roles in the form of an array.

## Time for action – checking to make sure the database is secure

Your _users database should be secure, so that only admins can read or alter the structure of the database. Let's quickly test this:

1.  Open **Terminal**.

2.  Try to read the user document again by running the following command. Again, replace your_username with the username of the service admin that you just created:

    ```
    curl localhost:5984/_users/org.couchdb.user:your_username
    ```

3.  **Terminal** will respond with the following:

    ```
    {"error":"unauthorized","reason":"You are not authorized to access this db."}
    ```

## What just happened?

With the CouchDB instance out of Admin Party mode, the authentication module stepped in to make sure that anonymous users couldn't read the database.

 We'll add more security to the databases down the road, but this is one of the simplest ways to add security to a database.

If you were to play around with the command line again, you would be restricted by doing anything with the _users database, but you would also notice that the test-db database is operating just as it was before, perfect! That's exactly what we wanted. You might be asking how do I access the _users database through the command line, now that security is enabled? You have to show that you are an admin by passing your credentials to the RESTful JSON API.

## Time for action – accessing a database with security enabled

Let's quickly try to access a database that has security enabled by passing the username and password with our request.

1. Open **Terminal**.

2. View all of the documents saved in the `_users` database by running the following command. Replace `username` and `password` with your admin's username and password.

```
curl username:password@localhost:5984/_users/_all_docs
```

3. **Terminal** will respond with the same data that you saw before you added the authentication.

```
{
    "_id": "org.couchdb.user:your_username",
    "_rev": "1-b9af54a7cdc392c2c298591f0dcd81f3",
    "name": "your_username",
    "password_sha": "3bc7d6d86da61fed6d4d82e1e4d1c3ca587aecc8",
    "roles": [],
    "salt": "9812acc4866acdec35c903f0cc072c1d",
    "type": "user"
}
```

## What just happened?

You just issued a GET request to the `_users` database and used the username and password of the server admin that we created earlier to authenticate us. Once authenticated, we were able to access the data normally. If you want to perform any action on a secure database, you just need to prepend `username:password@` before the URL of the resource you would like to work with.

## Pop quiz

1. What is the first sentence of CouchDB's definition according to `http://couchdb.apache.org/`?

2. What are the four verbs used by HTTP, and how does each match up to CRUD?

3. What is the URL to access Futon?

4. What does the term Admin Party mean to CouchDB, and how do you take CouchDB out of this mode?

5. How would you authenticate a user for a secure database through the command line?

# Summary

We learned a lot about CouchDB in this chapter. Let's quickly review:

♦ We defined CouchDB by looking at databases, documents, and the RESTful JSON API

♦ We compared CouchDB to a traditional relational database such as MySQL

♦ We interacted with CouchDB's RESTful JSON API, using `curl` statements

♦ We created and altered documents by using Futon

♦ We learned how to add security to a database and tested its effectiveness

Get ready! In the next chapter, we are going to start building the PHP framework that will be the platform on which we will develop in the rest of the book.

# 4

# Starting your Application

*We are ready to start developing the framework behind our application!*

In this chapter, we will:

- ◆ Create a simple PHP framework from scratch - Bones
- ◆ Learn how to use Git for source control
- ◆ Add functionality to Bones to handle URL requests
- ◆ Build out support for views and layouts, so that we can add a frontend to our application
- ◆ Add code to allow us to handle all of the HTTP methods
- ◆ Set up complex routing and build it into an example application
- ◆ Add the ability to use public files and use them with our framework
- ◆ Publish our code to GitHub, so that we can manage our source code

Let's jump right into it!

## What we'll build in this book

For the rest of this book, we will create a simple social network that is similar to Twitter. Let's call it Verge.

Verge will allow users to sign up, log in, and create posts. By building this application, we'll jump over the same hurdles that most developers do when they build an application, and we'll learn to rely on CouchDB for some of the heavy lifting.

In order to build Verge, we are going to make a light PHP wrapper that will handle the basic routing and HTTP requests that we mentioned in the previous chapter. Let's call this framework Bones.

# Bones

In this book, we are going to build a very lightweight framework called Bones to run our application. You will probably wonder to yourself *why are we building another framework?* It's a valid question! There are tons of PHP frameworks out there such as: Zend framework, Cake, Symfony, and so on. These are all powerful frameworks, but they also have a steep learning curve, and it would be impossible to touch on each of them in this book. Instead, we'll create an extremely light PHP framework that will help simplify our development but won't have a lot of other bells and whistles. By building this framework, you'll have a greater understanding of HTTP methods and how to build light applications from the ground up. Once you've developed this application using Bones, it should be easy for you to apply your knowledge to another framework, because we'll be using some pretty standard processes.

If you run into any problems through this chapter or are eager to see the finished product, then you can access the full Bones framework on GitHub: `https://github.com/timjuravich/bones`. I'll also cover an easy way for you to grab all of this code at the end of this chapter.

Let's get started by setting up our project.

# Project setup

In this section, we'll go through the steps of creating folders for our code and make sure that we initialize Git so that our source code can be tracked as we add new features to the project.

## Time for action – creating the directories for Verge

Let's begin the setup of our project by creating a directory in the `/Library/WebServer/Documents` folder, and name that directory `verge`. This directory will contain all of the code for your project. For the sake of brevity, throughout this chapter, we'll call `/Library/WebServer/Documents/verge` our **working** directory.

Inside our working directory, let's create four new folders for our source files to go into:

1.  Create a folder called `classes`. This folder will contain the PHP class objects that we'll be using in this project

2. Create a folder called `lib`. This folder will contain PHP libraries that our application relies on, which, in our case, will be the `Bones` framework and the class that will communicate with CouchDB.

3. Create a folder called `public`. This folder will contain all of our public files, such as **Cascading Style Sheets** (CSS), JavaScript, and images that our applications will need.

4. Create a folder called `views`. This folder will contain our layout and the different pages of our web application.

   If you were to look at your working directory, the end result of this section should look similar to the following screenshot:

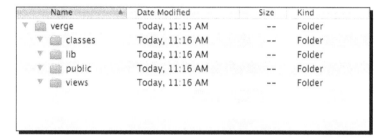

## What just happened?

We quickly created some placeholder folders for the organization of the code that we'll add throughout the rest of this book.

## Source control with Git

In order for us to keep track of our application, our progress, and to allow us to roll back if we make mistakes, we need to have source control on our repository up and running. We installed Git in *Chapter 2, Setting Up Your Development Environment*, so let's put it to good use. There are a few desktop clients out there that you can use, but we'll use the command line for simplicity, so that it works for everyone.

## Time for action – initializing a Git repository

Git needs to be initialized in the root of each development project so that it can keep a track of all of the project files. Let's do this for our newly created `verge` project!

1. Open **Terminal**.

2. Type the following command to change directories to our working directory:
   ```
   cd /Library/Webserver/Documents/verge/
   ```

**3.** Type the following command to initialize our Git directory:

```
git init
```

**4.** Git will respond with the following:

```
Initialized empty Git repository in /Library/WebServer/Documents/
verge/.git/
```

**5.** Keep your **Terminal** window open so that you can interact with Git in this chapter.

### What just happened?

We used **Terminal** to initialize our Git repository by using the command `git init` in our working directory. Git responded to let us know that everything went okay. Now that we have our Git repository set up, we'll need to add each file under source control when new ones are created. The syntax for adding a file to Git is simple, `git add path_to_file`. You can also add all of the files within a directory recursively with a wildcard statement by typing "`git add .`". In most parts of this chapter, we'll be quickly adding files, so we will use "`git add .`".

## Implementing basic routing

Before we start creating `Bones`, let's first look into why we'll need its help. Let's start by creating a simple file that will just make sure that our application is all set up and ready to go.

### Time for action – creating our first file: index.php

The first file we'll create is a file called `index.php`. This file will handle all of the requests to our application and eventually will be the main application controller that will talk to `Bones`.

**1.** Create `index.php` in the working directory, and add the following text:

```
<?php echo 'Welcome to Verge'; ?>
```

**2.** Open your browser, and go to the url: `http://localhost/verge/`.

**3.** The `index.php` file will display the following words:

```
Welcome to Verge
```

## *What just happened?*

We created a simple PHP file called `index.php` that simply returns text to us at this point. We can access this file only if we directly go to `http://localhost/verge/` or `http://localhost/verge/index.php`. However, our goal is that `index.php` will be hit for almost every request inside of our working directory (with the exception being our `public` files). In order for us to do this, we need to add a `.htaccess` file that will allow us to use URL rewriting.

## .htaccess files

`.htaccess` files are known as distributed configuration files, and they allow Apache configurations to be overridden on a directory basis. If you remember, in *Chapter 1, Introduction to CouchDB* we made sure that we could use the `.htaccess` files by changing some lines of code to `Override All`. Most PHP frameworks utilize the `.htaccess` files in the same way that we will, so it's important for you to get familiar with this process.

## Time for action – creating the .htaccess file

In order for us to handle all requests to a directory, we'll create a `.htaccess` file in the working directory.

1. Create a file called `.htaccess` in the working directory.

2. Add the following code to the file:

```
<IfModule mod_rewrite.c>
  RewriteEngine On
  RewriteCond %{REQUEST_FILENAME} !-f
  RewriteCond %{REQUEST_FILENAME} !-d
  RewriteRule ^(.*)$ index.php?request=$1 [QSA,L]
</IfModule>
```

3. Open the file `index.php` in the working directory.

4. Change the code inside of `index.php` to match the following:

```
<?php echo $_GET['request']; ?>
```

**5.** Open your browser, go to `http://localhost/verge/test/abc`, and go to `http://localhost/verge/test/123`. Notice that the page will respond back to you with the same value that you entered at the end of the root URL.

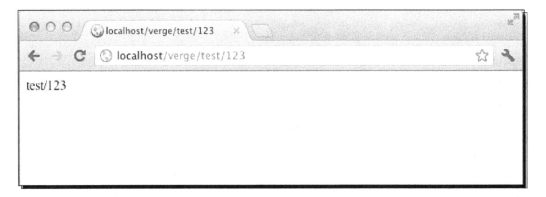

## *What just happened?*

We first created a `.htaccess` file to enable us to do URL rewriting. The first line, `<IfModule mod_rewrite.c>`, checks to make sure that we enabled the `mod_rewrite` module. This will be `true` because we enabled `mod_rewrite` in our `http.conf` file in *Chapter 2*.

The next line of the file says `RewriteEngine On`, and it does it exactly what you think it does; it turns Apache's `RewriteEngine` on and waits for some conditions and rules. Next, we set two `RewriteCond` (rewrite conditions). The first `RewriteCond` tells `RewriteEngine` to rewrite URLs if the passed URL does not match the location of an existing file (which is what the `-f` stands for). The second `RewriteCond` tells `RewriteEngine` to rewrite URLs that are not already an existing directory (which is what the `-d` stands for). Lastly, we set our `RewriteRule`, which says that when a URL is entered for the first value, forward it to the second value (target). This `RewriteRule` tells the `RewriteEngine` that any URL that is passed to this directory should be forced to go through the index file and passed the route to the `index.php` file in the form of a query string named `request`.

At the end, the string is `[QSA, L]`. Let me explain what this means. `QSA` means, if there are any query strings added to the request, append it to the rewrite target. `L` means, stop trying to find matches, and don't apply any more rules.

You then opened up the `index.php` file and changed the code to output the `request` variable. You now know that the route entered into the browser will be passed to the `index.php` file in the form of a query string.

With all of this code in place, we tested everything out, and by going to the URL `http://localhost/verge/test/abc`, our `index.php` file returned `test/abc`. When we changed the URL to `http://localhost/verge/test/123`, our `index.php` file returned `test/123` back to us.

# Hacking together URLs

At this point, we technically could scrap things together with a bunch of `if` statements, allowing our website to serve up different content. For example, we could show different content based on the URL, by just adding a few pieces of code into `index.php` as follows:

```
if ($_GET['request'] == '') {
  echo "Welcome To Verge";
} elseif ($_GET['request'] == 'signup') {
  echo "Sign Up!";
}
```

In this piece of code, if a user went to the URL `http://localhost/verge`, their browser would display:

`Welcome to Verge`

Likewise, if a user went to `http://localhost/verge/signup`, their browser would display:

`Sign Up!`

We could extend this way of thinking further and further, by writing a variety of `if` statements, stringing our code into one long file, and jumping right into programming our application. However, this would be an absolute nightmare to maintain, difficult to debug, and is just bad practice, in general.

Instead, let's delete all of the code in our `index.php` file and focus on building our project the right way. For the rest of this chapter, we'll work on creating a simple framework called `Bones`, which will handle some of the heavy lifting of requests for us.

# Creating the skeleton of Bones

As I've mentioned before, `Bones` is an extremely lightweight framework consisting of a little over 100 lines of code in all, which resides in one file. In this section, we'll begin to form the structure onto which we will build more and more functionality in the following sections.

# Time for action – hooking up our application to Bones

Let's start by creating the Bones library and then connecting our index.php file to it.

**1.** Create a file named bones.php inside of the lib folder of our working directory (/Library/Webserver/Documents/verge/lib/bones.php).

**2.** Add the following code to the index.php file in our working directory, so that we can talk to the newly created bones.php file:

```php
<?php
  include 'lib/bones.php';
```

## What just happened?

All that this code is doing is including our lib/bones.php file, and that's good enough for us right now! Notice that we didn't end the file with a ?>, as you may be accustomed to seeing. The ?> tag is actually optional, and, in our case, leaving it will allow us to reduce the unwanted whitespace and to add headers to response later in the code, if we would like.

## Using Bones to handle requests

To illustrate what we are planning to do with the Bones class, let's go through a quick example on what we would like to accomplish by the end of this section.

◆ If a browser was to hit the URL http://localhost/verge/signup, we want Bones to intercept the call and interpret it as http://localhost/verge/index.php?request=signup.

◆ Bones will then look through a list of routes that we've defined in our index.php file and see if there's a match.

◆ If there is indeed a match, Bones will perform a callback to the matching function and execute the actions inside of that route.

If any of that was confusing, don't worry. Hopefully it'll start to make sense as we slowly build this functionality.

# Time for action – creating the class structure of Bones

Let's start building out the `Bones` class by adding the following code to the `lib/bones.php` file inside our working directory:

`/Library/Webserver/Documents/verge/lib/bones.php`

```php
<?php

  class Bones {
    private static $instance;
    public static $route_found = false;
    public $route = '';

    public static function get_instance() {
      if (!isset(self::$instance)) {
        self::$instance = new Bones();
      }

      return self::$instance;
  }
```

## What just happened?

We just created our `Bones` class, added a few `private` and `public` variables, and a strange function called `get_instance()`. The private static variable `$instance`, mixed with the function `get_instance()`, forms something that is called **The Singleton Pattern**.

The Singleton Pattern allows our `Bones` class to not just be a simple class, but also to be one object. This means that each time we call our `Bones` class, we are accessing a single existing object. But if the object does not exist, it will create a new one for us to use. It's a bit of a complex idea; however, I hope it starts to make sense as we make use of it down the road.

## Accessing the route

Now that we have the basic concept of our class, let's add some functions to grab and interpret the route (URL that was passed to `Bones`) each time a new request is created. We will then compare the result against each possible route in the next section.

## Time for action – creating functions to access the route on Bones creation

In order for us to figure out what route was passed in a request, we'll need to add the following two functions to the `lib/bones.php` file underneath the closing bracket of the `get_instance()` function:

/Library/Webserver/Documents/verge/lib/bones.php

```
public static function get_instance() {
  if (!isset(self::$instance)) {
    self::$instance = new Bones();
  }

  return self::$instance;
}

public function __construct() {
  $this->route = $this->get_route();
}

protected function get_route() {
  parse_str($_SERVER['QUERY_STRING'], $route);
  if ($route) {
    return '/' . $route['request'];
  } else {
    return '/';
  }
}
```

### What just happened?

In this piece of code, we added a function called `__construct()`, which is a function that is automatically called each time a class is created. Our `__construct()` function then calls another function named `get_route()`, which will grab the route (if there is one) from our request query string and return it to the instance's `route` variable.

### Matching URLs

In order for us to match up the routes of our application, we will need to push each possible route through a function called `register`.

# Time for action – creating the register function to match routes

The `register` function will be one of the most important functions in the `Bones` class down the road, but we'll just get started by adding the following code at the end of our `lib/bones.php` file:

/Library/Webserver/Documents/verge/lib/bones.php

```
public static function register($route, $callback) {
  $bones = static::get_instance();

  if ($route == $bones->route && !static::$route_found) {
    static::$route_found = true;
    echo $callback($bones);
  } else {
    return false;
  }
}
```

## What just happened?

We started by creating a public static function called `register`. This function has two parameters: `$route` and `$callback`. `$route` contains the route that we are attempting to match against the actual route, and `$callback` is the function that will be executed if the routes do match. Notice that, at the start of the `register` function, we call for our `Bones` instance, using the `static:get_instance()` function. This is the Singleton Pattern in action, returning the single instance of the `Bones` object to us.

The `register` function then checks to see if the route that we visited through our browser matches the route that was passed into the function. If there is a match, our `$route_found` variable will be set to `true`, which will allow us to skip looking through the rest of the routes. The `register` function will then execute a callback function that will do the work that was defined in our route. Our `Bones` instance will also be passed with the callback function, so that we can use it to our advantage. If the route is not a match, we will return `false` so that we know the route wasn't a match.

We are now at the end of what we'll do in `Bones` for now. So, make sure to end your class with a closing bracket as follows:

```
}
```

## Calling the register function from our application

We now have a basic understanding of what Bones is supposed to do, but we're missing a function that will tie our index.php and lib/bones.php files together. We'll eventually create four functions that will do this, one for each HTTP method. But, for now, let's just create our get function.

## Time for action – creating a get function in our Bones class

Let's create a get function at the top of the lib/bones.php file, right after the <?php tag and before we define the Bones class:

/Library/Webserver/Documents/verge/lib/bones.php

```php
<?php

ini_set('display_errors','On');
error_reporting(E_ERROR | E_PARSE);

function get($route, $callback) {
  Bones::register($route, $callback);
}

class Bones {
...
}
```

### What just happened?

This function lies in the lib/bones.php file and is called for each get route that you have defined in your index.php file. This function is a simple pass-through function that hands off the route and callback to the register function of Bones.

Are we on the same page?

We did a whole lot in this section. Let's double check that your code matches my code:

/Library/Webserver/Documents/verge/lib/bones.php

```php
<?php

function get($route, $callback) {
  Bones::register($route, $callback);
}
```

```php
class Bones {
  private static $instance;
  public static $route_found = false;
  public $route = '';

  public function __construct() {
    $this->route = $this->get_route();
  }

  public static function get_instance() {
    if (!isset(self::$instance)) {
      self::$instance = new Bones();
    }
    return self::$instance;
  }

  public static function register($route, $callback) {
    $bones = static::get_instance();

    if ($route == $bones->route && !static::$route_found) {
      static::$route_found = true;
      echo $callback($bones);
    } else {
      return false;
    }
  }

  protected function get_route() {
    parse_str($_SERVER['QUERY_STRING'], $route);
    if ($route) {
      return '/' . $route['request'];
    } else {
      return '/';
    }
  }

}
```

## Adding routes to our application

We are finished with our `lib/bones.php` file for now. All we need to do is add a few routes to our `index.php` file that call the `get` function that lives in the `lib/bones.php` folder.

## Time for action – creating routes for us to test against Bones

Open up the `index.php` file and add the following two routes so that we can test our new code:

```php
<?php
include 'lib/bones.php';

get('/', function($app) {
  echo "Home";
});

get('/signup', function($app) {
  echo "Signup!";
});
```

### What just happened?

We just created two routes for our `Bones` class to handle / (which is the root URL) and `/signup`.

There are a few things to notice in the code that we just added:

- Our two `get` routes are now clean, little functions, including our route and a function that will act as our callback function
- Once the function is executed, we are using `echo` to display the simple text
- When a route is matched and a callback is executed from `Bones`, the instance of `Bones` is returned as the variable `$app`, which can be used anywhere in the callback function

### Testing it out!

We're all set to test out our new additions to `Bones`! Open up your browser, and go to `http://localhost/verge/`. You'll see the word `Home`. Then direct your browser to `http://localhost/verge/signup`, and you'll see the text `Signup!`

While our application is still very basic, I hope you see the strength in adding routes in this simple fashion. Feel free to play around and add a few more routes before moving on to the next section.

### Adding changes to Git

In this section, we started our `lib/bones.php` library and added some simple routing. Let's add all of our changes to Git so that we can track our progress.

1. Open **Terminal**.

2. Type the following command to change directories to our working directory:

```
cd /Library/Webserver/Documents/verge/
```

3. Add all of the files that we've created in this directory by typing the following command:

```
git add .
```

4. Give Git a description of what we've done since our last commit:

```
git commit -am 'Created bones.php and added simple support for routing'
```

# Handling layouts and views

We're going to take a break from routes for a bit and add some fun frontend functionality. Every application consists of a number of pages which we'll call **views**. Each view has a standard layout that these views will populate. Layouts are a wrapper for views and may contain links to CSS references, navigation, or whatever else you think makes sense to be common to each view.

## Using Bones to support views and layouts

In order to support views and layouts, we will need to add some additional functionality to our Bones class.

## Time for action – using constants to get the location of the working directory

The first thing that we need to do is create a named constant called ROOT, which will give us the full location of our working directory. Until now, we haven't had to do any extra including of files, but with our layouts and views, it'll start to get a bit difficult if we don't add some functionality to get the working directory. In order to support this, let's add a simple line of code right at the top of our lib/bones.php file.

```php
<?php

ini_set('display_errors','On');
error_reporting(E_ERROR | E_PARSE);

define('ROOT', __DIR__ . '/..');

function get($route, $callback) {
...
}
```

## What just happened?

This line of code creates a constant named ROOT that we can then use throughout our code to reference the working directory. \_\_DIR\_\_ gives us the root of the current file (/Library/Webserver/Documents/verge/lib). So, we'll want to look at one more directory back by appending /.. to the path.

## Time for action – allowing Bones to store variables and the content path

We need to be able to set and receive variables to our views from index.php. So, let's add that support into Bones.

1. Let's define a public array called $vars that will allow us to store variables from our routes in index.php and a string called $content that will house the path to the view that will be loaded into our layout. We'll start by adding two variables just inside our lib/bones.php class:

```
class Bones {
public $route = '';
public $content = '';
public $vars = array();

public function __construct() {
...
}
```

2. In order for us to set variables from our index.php file, we'll create a simple function called set that will allow us to pass an index and a value for a variable and save it to the current Bones instance. Let's create a function in lib/bones.php called set, right after the get_route() function.

```
protected function get_route() {
...
}

public function set($index, $value) {
  $this->vars[$index] = $value;
}
```

## What just happened?

We added two new variables, $vars and $content, to our Bones class. Both of them will be utilized in the next section. We then created a set function to allow us to send variables to our Bones class from our index.php file so that we can display them in our views.

Next, we need to add the ability for us to call views from index.php and have them displayed. The function that will house this functionality will be called render.

## Time for action – allowing our application to display a view by calling it in index.php

We'll start by creating a public function, called render that accepts two arguments. The first is $view, which is the name (or path) of the view you want to display, and the second is $layout, which will define which layout we use to show the view. Layout will also have a default value, so that we can keep things simple, in order to handle the displaying of views. Add the following code to the lib/bones.php file, right after the set function:

```
public function set($index, $value) {
  $this->vars[$index] = $value;
}

public function render($view, $layout = "layout") {
  $this->content = ROOT. '/views/' . $view . '.php';
  foreach ($this->vars as $key => $value) {
    $$key = $value;
  }

  if (!$layout) {
    include($this->content);
  } else {
    include(ROOT. '/views/' . $layout . '.php');
  }
}
```

## What just happened?

We created the `render` function that will set the path of the view that we want to display in our layout. All of the views will be saved inside the `views` directory that we created earlier in this chapter. The code then loops through each of the variables set in the instance's `vars` array. For each variable, we use a strange syntax $$, which allows us to set a variable using the key we defined in our array. This will allow us to reference the variables directly in our views. Finally, we added a simple `if` statement that checks to see if a `layout` file is defined. If `$layout` is not defined, we'll simply return the content of the view. If `$layout` is defined, we'll include the layout, which will return our view wrapped in the defined layout. We do this so that we can avoid using layouts down the road, if we want. For instance, in an AJAX call, we might just want to return the view without the layout.

## Time for action – creating a simple layout file

In this section, we'll create a simple layout file called `layout.php`. Remember that in our `render` function, there is a default value for `$layout`, and that is set to `layout`. This means that, by default, Bones will look for `views/layout.php`. So, let's create that file now.

1.  Start by creating a new file in our `views` directory called `layout.php`.

2.  Add the following code in the newly created `views/layout.php`:

```html
<html>
  <body>
    <h1>Verge</h1>
    <?php include($this->content); ?>
  </body>
</html>
```

## What just happened?

We created a very simple HTML layout that will be used in all of our views in the application. If you remember, our `render` function in `Bones` uses the path set as the `$content` variable that we set in the previous function and also includes it, so that we can display the view.

## Adding views to our application

Now that we have all of the pieces in place for views, we just need to add a few lines of code to the `index.php` file, so that we can render views.

# Time for action – rendering views inside of our routes

Let's replace the existing portions of code inside our routes that just echoed out text with the following code that will actually use our new framework:

```
get('/', function($app) {
  $app->set('message', 'Welcome Back!');
  $app->render('home');
});

get('/signup', function($app) {
  $app->render('signup');
});
```

## What just happened?

For the root route, we used our new function `set` to pass a variable with the key of `'message'` and its contents being `'Welcome Back!'`, and we then told `Bones` to render the home view. For the `signup` route, we are just rendering the `signup` view.

# Time for action – creating views

We are just about ready to test this new code out, but we need to create the actual views so that we can display them.

1. Start by creating two new files in the `views` folder, inside our working directory, called `home.php` and `signup.php`.

2. Add the following code to the `views/home.php` file by writing the following code:
```
Home Page <br /><br />
<?php echo $message; ?>
```

3. Add the following code to the `views/signup.php` file:
```
Signup Now!
```

## What just happened?

We created two simple views that will be rendered by the `index.php` file. The line of code inside `views/home.php` that says `<?php echo $message; ?>`, will display the variable with the name message that was passed to our `Bones` library from our `index.php` file. Test it out!

Open up your browser, go to `http://localhost/verge/` or `http://localhost/verge/signup`, and you'll see that all of our hard work has paid off. Our layout is now rendering, and our views are being displayed. We were also able to pass a variable, called `message`, from `index.php` and output the value on our home view. I hope you can start to see the strength of what we are adding to `Bones` so far!

## Adding changes to Git

So far, we added support for layouts and views, which will help us build out all of the pages of our application. Let's add all of our changes to Git, so that we can track our progress.

1. Open **Terminal**.

2. Type the following command to change directories to our working directory:

   `cd /Library/Webserver/Documents/verge/`

3. Add all of the files that we've created in this directory, by typing the following command:

   `git add .`

4. Give Git a description of what we've done since our last commit:

   `git commit -am 'Added support for views and layouts'`

# Adding support for other HTTP methods

Until now, we've been handling GET calls, but in a web application, we will have to be able to support all of the HTTP methods that we have talked about in the previous chapter: GET, PUT, POST, and DELETE.

## Time for action – retrieving the HTTP method used in a request

We have done most of the heavy lifting required to support, capture, and handle HTTP requests. We just need to plug in a few extra lines of code.

1. Let's add a variable to our `Bones` class, called `$method`, after our `$route` variable. This variable will store the HTTP method that was performed on each request:

```
class Bones {
  private static $instance;
  public static $route_found = false;
  public $route = '';
  public $method = '';
  public $content = '';
```

2. In order for us to get the method on each request, we will need to add a line of code in our __construct() function, named get_route(), and save the value of the result in our instances variable $method. This means that when Bones is created on each request, it will also retrieve the method and save it to our Bones instance, so that we can use it down the road. Do this by adding the following code:

```
public function __construct() {
  $this->route = $this->get_route();
  $this->method = $this->get_method();
}
```

3. Let's create the function called get_method(), so that our __construct() function can call it. Let's add it right after our get_route() method:

```
protected function get_route() {
  parse_str($_SERVER['QUERY_STRING'], $route);
  if ($route) {
    return '/' . $route['request'];
  } else {
    return '/';
  }
}

protected function get_method() {
  return isset($_SERVER['REQUEST_METHOD']) ?   $_SERVER['REQUEST_
METHOD'] : 'GET';
}
```

## What just happened?

We added a variable $method to your Bones class. This variable is set by the function get_route(), and returns a value to the instances $method variable each time a request is made to Bones through the __construct() method. That probably sounds super confusing, but bear with me.

The get_route() function uses an array called $_SERVER that is created by the web server, and allows us to retrieve information on request and execution. This simple one liner is saying that if REQUEST_METHOD is set in $_SERVER, then return it, but if REQUEST_METHOD is not set for whatever reason, just return GET for the method to be safe.

# Time for action – altering the register to support different methods

Now that we are retrieving the method on each request, we need to alter our register function so that we can pass $method along with each of our routes in order for them to match properly.

*1.* Add $method onto the register function in lib/bones.php so that we can pass a method into the function:

```php
public static function register($route, $callback, $method) {
  $bones = static::get_instance();
```

*2.* We now need to update our simple route matching in our register function to also check that the passed routes $method matches our instance variables $bones->method, which is the method that actually happened on the server:

```php
public static function register($route, $callback, $method) {
  $bones = static::get_instance();

  if ($route == $bones->route && !static::
    $route_found && $bones->method == $method) {
     static::$route_found = true;
     echo $callback($bones);
  } else {
     return false;
  }
}
```

## What just happened?

We added a $method argument to be passed into our register function. We then used this $method variable in our register function by adding it to the list of arguments that have to be true in order for a route to be considered a match. Therefore, if the routes match, but if it's a different HTTP method than expected, it will be ignored. This will allow you to create routes with the same name but act differently based on the method that is passed. Sounds just like REST, which we talked about in the previous chapter, doesn't it?

In order to execute the register functions, let's look back at the get function that we have at the beginning of our lib/bones.php file:

```php
<?php

ini_set('display_errors','On');
error_reporting(E_ERROR | E_PARSE);

define('ROOT', dirname(dirname(__FILE__)));

function get($route, $callback) {
  Bones::register($route, $callback);
}
```

Hopefully, it should be pretty easy to see what we're going to do next. Let's expand our current `get` function and create three more functions, one for each of the remaining HTTP methods, making sure we pass in each method's name in caps.

```php
<?php

ini_set('display_errors','On');
error_reporting(E_ERROR | E_PARSE);

define('ROOT', dirname(dirname(__FILE__)));

function get($route, $callback) {
  Bones::register($route, $callback, 'GET');
}

function post($route, $callback) {
  Bones::register($route, $callback, 'POST');
}

function put($route, $callback) {
  Bones::register($route, $callback, 'PUT');
}

function delete($route, $callback) {
  Bones::register($route, $callback, 'DELETE');
}
```

We have added all of the functionality needed in our Bones library to allow us to use other HTTP methods, pretty simple right?

## Time for action – adding simple but powerful helpers to Bones

Let's add two little functions to our `lib/bones.php` file that will help us use forms.

1. Add a function called `form` that looks as follows:

```php
public function form($key) {
  return $_POST[$key];
}
```

2. Add a function called `make_route`. This function will allow our `Bones` instance to create clean links so that we can link to other resources in our application:

```php
public function make_route($path = '') {
  $url = explode("/", $_SERVER['PHP_SELF']);
  if ($url[1] == "index.php") {
    return $path;
  } else {
    return '/' . $url[1] . $path;
  }
}
```

## What just happened?

We added a simple function called form that serves as a wrapper around the $_POST array, which is an array of variables passed through the HTTP POST method. This will allow us to collect values after we POST them. The next function we created is called make_route. This function will soon be used everywhere to create clean links so that we can link to other resources in our application.

## Using a form to test our HTTP method support

We've added some cool stuff here. Let's move on to test the support of the newly added HTTP methods.

Open up the file verge/views/signup.php, and add a simple form, similar to the following:

```
Signup

<form action="<?php echo $this->make_route('/signup') ?>"
  method="post">
  <label for="name">Name</label>
  <input id="name" name="name" type="text"> <br />
  <input type="Submit" value="Submit">
</form>
```

We set the form's action attribute by using $this->make_route. $this->make_route used our Bones instance to make a route that would resolve to our signup route. We then defined the method as using the post method. The rest of the form is pretty standard with a label and textbox for name, and a submit button to process the form.

If you were to go in your browser to http://localhost/verge/signup, you would now see the form, but if you click on the submit button, you will be sent to a blank page. This is because we haven't yet defined our post method in our index.php file.

Open up the index.php file, and add the following code:

```
get('/signup', function($app) {
  $app->render('signup');
});

post('/signup', function($app) {
  $app->set('message', 'Thanks for Signing Up ' .
    $app->form('name') . '!');
  $app->render('home');
});
```

Let's walk through this piece of code and make sure it's clear what we're doing here. We're telling `Bones` to look for the route `/signup` with a `post` method being sent to it. Once this route is resolved, the callback will set the value of a variable `message` with some text. The text includes the new function we created called `$app->form('name')`. This function is grabbing the posted value from the form with the attribute `name`. We are then going to tell `Bones` to render the home view, allowing us to see the message.

# Testing it out!

Let's try all of this out now!

1. Open up your browser, and go to: `http://localhost/verge/signup`.
2. Your browser should show the following:

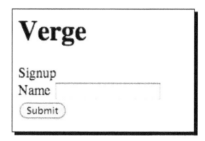

3. Enter your name (I entered `Tim`), and click on **Submit**.

# Adding changes to Git

In this section, we added support for all of the HTTP methods, which will allow us to handle any type of requests. Let's add all of our changes to Git, so that we can track our progress.

1. Open **Terminal**.
2. Type the following command to change directories to our working directory:

   `cd /Library/Webserver/Documents/verge/`

3. Add all of the files that we created in this directory by typing the following command:

   ```
   git add .
   ```

4. Give Git a description of what we've done since our last commit:

   ```
   git commit -am 'Added support for all HTTP methods'
   ```

# Adding support for complex routing

Our framework is technically all ready for us to start building on top. However, we don't have enough support to match and handle complex routes. Since most applications will need this, let's quickly add it.

## Handling complex routes

For example, in the `index.php` file, we'll want to be able to define a route for a user profile. This route might be `/user/:username`. In this case, `:username` will be a variable that we can then access. So, if you went to the URL `/user/tim`, you could access the username `tim` by using `Bones` to grab that section of the URL, and return its value.

Let's start by adding another variable and another call in our `__construct` function to our `lib/bones.php` file:

```
public $content = '';
public $vars = array();
public $route_segments = array();
public $route_variables = array();

public function __construct() {
  $this->route = $this->get_route();
  $this->route_segments = explode('/', trim($this->route, '/'));
  $this->method = $this->get_method();
}
```

We just added two variables to our `Bones` instance called `$route_segments` and `$route_variables`. `$route_segments` is set each time the `Bones` object is created using `__construct()`. The `$route_segments` array splits `$route` into usable segments by splitting them on a slash (`/`). This will allow us to examine the URL that the browser sends to `Bones`, and then decide if the route matches. `$route_variables` will be a library of variables that were passed in through the route, and it will enable us to use the `index.php` file.

Now, let's start doctoring up the `register` function so that we can handle these special routes. Let's remove all of the code that's in there, and slowly add some code back.

```
public static function register($route, $callback, $method) {
  if (!static::$route_found) {
    $bones = static::get_instance();
    $url_parts = explode('/', trim($route, '/'));
    $matched = null;
```

We added an `if` statement that checked to see if the route has already matched. If it has, we just ignore everything else in the `register` function. Then, we added `$url_parts`. This will split up the route that we pass into the register function, and will help us compare this route against the actual route the browser hit.

>  We'll be closing the `if` statement and register function when we finish up this section; don't forget to do that!

Let's start to compare `$bones->route_segments`, which is the route that the browser hit, against `$url_parts`, which is the route that we are trying to match. First, let's check to make sure that `$route_segments` and `$url_parts` are the same length. This will make sure that we save time by not digging deeper into the function, since we already know it doesn't match.

Add the following code into our `register` function in `lib/bones.php`:

```
if (count($bones->route_segments) == count($url_parts)) {

} else {
  // Routes are different lengths
  $matched = false;
}
```

Now, let's add a `for` loop inside the `if` statement that will loop each of the `$url_parts`, and try to match it against `route_segments`.

```
if (count($bones->route_segments) == count($url_parts)) {
  foreach ($url_parts as $key=>$part) {

  }
} else {
  // Routes are different lengths
  $matched = false;
}
```

In order to identify variables, we'll check for the existence of a colon (`:`). This represents the fact that this segment contains a variable value.

```
if (count($bones->route_segments) == count($url_parts)) {
  foreach ($url_parts as $key=>$part) {
    if (strpos($part, ":") !== false) {
      // Contains a route variable
    } else {
      // Does not contain a route variable
    }
  }
} else {
  // Routes are different lengths
  $matched = false;
}
```

Next, let's add a line of code that will take the value of the segment and save it into our `$route_variables` array, allowing us to use it later. Just because we found one matching variable, it does not mean that the whole route is a match, so we aren't going to set `$matched = true` just yet.

```
if (strpos($part, ":") !== false) {
  // Contains a route variable
  $bones->route_variables[substr($part, 1)] =
    $bones->route_segments[$key];
} else {
  // Does not contain a route variable
}
```

Let's break the line of code that we just added down. The second part, `$bones->route_segments[$key]`, is grabbing the value of the segment that was passed to the browser and has the same index as the segment we are currently looping through.

Then, `$bones->route_variables[substr($part, 1)]` saves the value into the `$route_variables` array with the index set to the `$part` value and then uses `substr` to make sure that we don't include the colon in the key.

This piece of code is a bit confusing. So, let's just go through a quick use case:

1. Open up your browser, and enter the URL `/users/tim`.
2. This register route starts checking the route `/users/:username`.
3. `$bones->route_segments[$key]` would return `tim`.
4. `$bones->route_variables[substr($part, 1)]` would save the value with the index username, enabling us later retrieve the value `tim`.

Now, let's finish off this if statement by inspecting the segments that do not contain route variables (the `else` part of the `if` statement). In this area, we are going to check to make sure that the segment we are checking matches the segment that was passed from the URL of the browser.

```
} else {
  // Does not contain a route variable
  if ($part == $bones->route_segments[$key]) {
    if (!$matched) {
      // Routes match
      $matched = true;
    }
  } else {
    // Routes don't match
    $matched = false;
  }
}
```

The code we just added checks to see if the value we were looping through $part matches the parallel segment in $route_segments. We then check to see if we've already marked this route as not matching. This shows us that we've already marked it as not matching in a previous segment check. If the routes do not match, we are going to set $matched = false. This will tell us that the URLs do not match, and we can ignore the rest of the route.

Let's add the final piece to the routing matching puzzle. This statement will look quite a bit similar to our old matching statement, but it will actually be quite a bit cleaner.

```
if (!$matched || $bones->method != $method) {
  return false;
} else {
  static::$route_found = true;
  echo $callback($bones);
}
```

This piece of code checks to make sure that our route matches in the matching statements above, by looking at the $matched variable. Then, we check to see that the HTTP method matches the route we check. If there is no match, we return `false` and exit out of this function. If there is a match, we set $route_found = true, and then perform a callback on the route, which will execute the code inside of the route defined in the `index.php` file.

Finally, let's just close out the if $route_found statement and the `register` function by adding the closing brackets to end this function.

```
  }
}
```

We added a lot of code in the past section. So, check to make sure your code matches up with what I have:

```
public static function register($route, $callback, $method) {
  if (!static::$route_found) {
    $bones = static::get_instance();
    $url_parts = explode('/', trim($route, '/'));
    $matched = null;

    if (count($bones->route_segments) == count($url_parts)) {
      foreach ($url_parts as $key=>$part) {
        if (strpos($part, ":") !== false) {
          // Contains a route variable
          $bones->route_variables[substr($part, 1)] = $bones->
            route_segments[$key];
        } else {
          // Does not contain a route variable
          if ($part == $bones->route_segments[$key]) {
            if (!$matched) {
              // Routes match
              $matched = true;
            }
          } else {
            // Routes don't match
            $matched = false;
          }
        }
      }
    } else {
      // Routes are different lengths
      $matched = false;
    }

    if (!$matched || $bones->method != $method) {
      return false;
    } else {
      static::$route_found = true;
      echo $callback($bones);
    }
  }
}
```

# Accessing route variables

Now that we are saving the route variables into an array, we need to add a function called request into the lib/bones.php file:

```
public function request($key) {
  return $this->route_variables[$key];
}
```

This function accepts a variable called $key and returns the value of the object in our route_variables array by returning the value with that same key.

# Adding more complex routes to index.php

We've done a lot of hard work. Let's test to make sure that it all went smoothly.

Let's add a quick route to index.php to test out the route variables:

```
get('/say/:message', function($app) {
  $app->set('message', $app->request('message'));
  $app->render('home');
});
```

We added a route with a route variable message. When the route was found and executed through the callback, we set a variable message to the value of the route variable message. Then, we rendered the home page, just as we've done a few times before.

# Testing it out!

If you open your browser and access the URL http://localhost/verge/say/hello, the browser will display: hello.

If you change the value to anything different, it will display the same value right back to you.

# Adding changes to Git

This section added more detailed route matching and allowed us to have route variables in our URLs. Let's add all of our changes to Git so that we can track our progress.

1.  Open **Terminal**.
2.  Type the following command to change directories to our working directory:
    ```
    cd /Library/Webserver/Documents/verge/
    ```

3. Add all of the files that we created in this directory by typing the following command:

```
git add .
```

4. Give Git a description of what we've done since our last commit:

```
git commit -am 'Refactored route matching to handle more complex
URLs and allow for route variables'
```

# Adding support for public files

An important part of developing web applications is the ability to use CSS and JS files. Currently, we really don't have a good way to use and display them. Let's change that!

## Time for action – altering .htaccess to support public files

We need to alter the `.htaccess` file, so that the request for the `public` files is not passed to the `index.php` file, but instead goes into to the `public` folder and finds the requested resource.

*1.* Start by opening up the .htaccess file that's in the root of our project.

*2.* Add the following highlighted code:

```
<IfModule mod_rewrite.c>
  RewriteEngine On

  RewriteCond %{REQUEST_FILENAME} !-f
  RewriteCond %{REQUEST_FILENAME} !-d
  RewriteRule ^css/([^/]+) public/css/$1 [L]
  RewriteRule ^js/([^/]+) public/js/$1 [L]

  RewriteCond %{REQUEST_FILENAME} !-f
  RewriteCond %{REQUEST_FILENAME} !-d
  RewriteRule ^(.*)$ index.php?request=$1 [QSA,L]
</IfModule>
```

## What just happened?

We just added `RewriteRule` to bypass our "catch all" rule that directs all requests if it's a `public` file. We then simplify the route to allow the URL to resolve to /css and /js instead of /public/css and /public/js.

We're ready to use public files. We just need to implement them, which should be just as easy as setting it up.

## Time for action – creating a stylesheet for the application

Let's start by adding a stylesheet to change the look of our application.

1.  Open `views/layout.php`. This file currently drives the layout for all of the pages in our project. We just need to add code to include our stylesheet:

```
<html>
  <head>
    <link href="<?php echo $this->make_route('/css/master.css') ?>"
      rel="stylesheet" type="text/css" />
  </head>
  <body>
    <?php include($this->view_content); ?>
  </body>
</html>
```

2.  Create a new file named `master.css`, and place it in our working directory's `public/css` folder.

3.  Add a quick piece of code to `public/css/master.css` that will display a different color background, so that we can test that this all works.

```
body {background:#e4e4e4;}
```

### What just happened?

We added a reference to a new stylesheet for our application called `master.css`. We used the standard markup to include a stylesheet, and used one of the functions of `Bones`, `make_route`, to properly create the path to the file.

Let's test to make sure our stylesheet is now being displayed properly.

1.  Open up your browser, and go to `http://localhost/verge/`.

2.  Your browser should show the following:

3.  Notice that the background color of our page has changed to grey, showing that the stylesheet has kicked in!

## Adding changes to Git

In this section, we added support for public files such as stylesheet, JavaScript, and images. We then tested it out by creating a `master.css` file. Let's add all of our changes to Git, so that we can track our progress.

1. Open **Terminal**.

2. Type the following command to change directories to our working directory:

   ```
   cd /Library/Webserver/Documents/verge/
   ```

3. Add all of the files that we created in this directory by typing the following command:

   ```
   git add .
   ```

4. Give Git a description of what we've done since our last commit:

   ```
   git commit -am 'Added clean routes for public files, created a
   master.css file, linked to master.css in layout.php'
   ```

# Publishing your code to GitHub

Now that we've created our framework and all of the underlying code, we can push our code to any service provider that supports Git. In this book, we'll use **GitHub**.

You can create an account on GitHub by going to: `https://github.com/plans`. GitHub has a variety of plans that you can choose from, but I recommend you pick the free account, so that you don't have to pay anything at this time. If you already have an account, you can log in and skip the creation of a new account.

Click on **Create a free account**.

 It's important to note that, by choosing a free account, all of your repositories will be `public`. This means that anyone will be able to see your code. This is fine for now, but as you get further in development, you might want to register for a paid account, so that it's not publicly available.

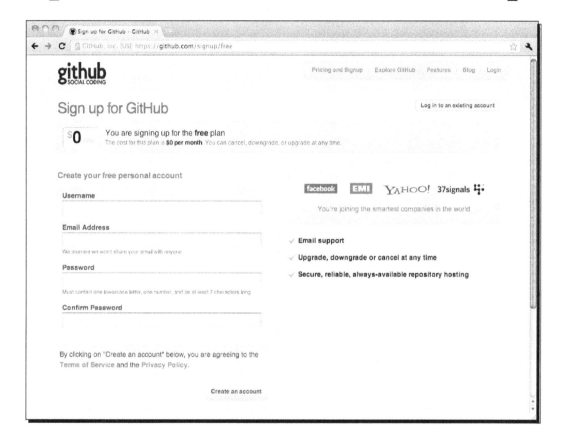

You will be shown a quick signup form. Fill it out completely, and click on **Create an account** when you are done.

With your account created, you will be shown your account dashboard. On this screen, you will see any activity on your account or repositories that you are watching. Since we do not yet have any repositories, we should start by clicking on **New Repository**.

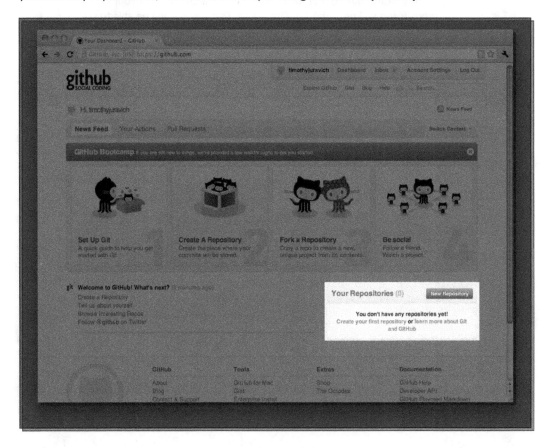

The **Create A New Repository** page will allow you to make a new repository for your code to live in.

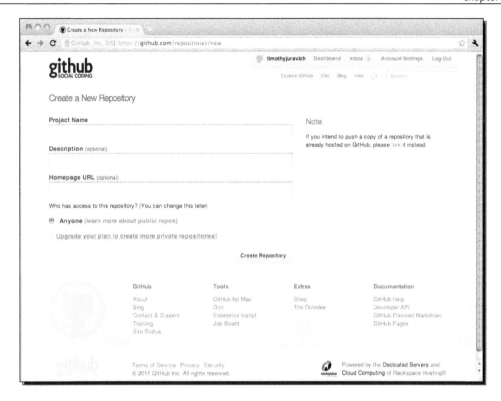

Complete the rest of this form by filling in each field.

◆ **Project Name**: verge

◆ **Description**: A social network called verge built using Bones

◆ **Homepage URL**: You can leave this blank for now

◆ Click on **Create Repository**

Your repository is now created and ready for you to push your code to. All you need to do is run a few statements in **Terminal**.

1. Open **Terminal**.

2. Type the following command to change directories to our working directory:
   ```
   cd /Library/WebServer/Documents/verge/
   ```

3. Add GitHub as your remote repository by entering the following command and replacing **username** with your GitHub username:
   ```
   git remote add origin git@github.com:username/verge.git
   ```

4.  Push your local repository to GitHub.

    ```
    git push -u origin master
    ```

5.  Git will return a bunch of text and will stop when it's complete.

If refresh the URL of your Git repository on `https://github.com` (my URL is `https://github.com/timjuravich/verge`), you will see all of your files, and if you click on **history** you will see all of the changes that you have added in each section as we've gone through this chapter.

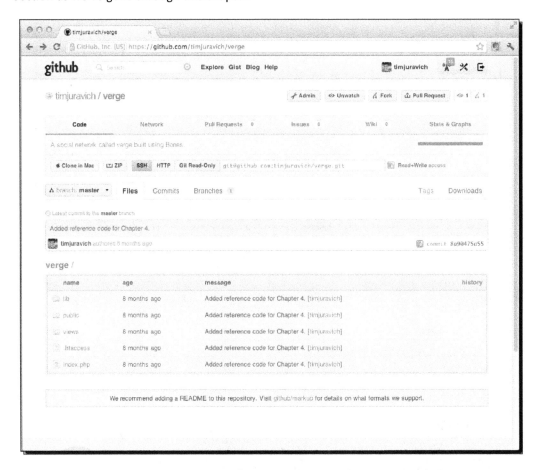

As you start adding more code, you have to manually push your code to GitHub each time by performing the command `git push origin master`. We'll continue to add to this repository as we go through this book.

# Get complete code from GitHub

If somewhere along the way you got lost, or weren't able to get everything working exactly like it should, you can easily clone Bones from a Git repository from GitHub, and you'll have a fresh copy with all of the changes we've made in this chapter.

1. Open **Terminal**.

2. Use the following command to change directories to our working directory:

   ```
   cd /Library/WebServer/Documents
   ```

3. Clone the repository to your local machine by typing the following command:

   ```
   git clone git@github.com:timjuravich/bones.git
   ```

4. Git will grab all of the files from GitHub, and move them to your local machine.

# Summary

We have done a tremendous amount of work in this chapter! We have:

- Created a PHP framework from scratch to handle web requests

- Added functionality for clean URLs, route variables, HTTP method support, a simple view and layout engine, and a system to display `public` files such as stylesheets, JavaScript, and images

- Tested each part our framework with our browser to make sure we could access our changes

- Published our code to GitHub so that we can see our changes and manage our code

Get ready! In the next chapter, we're going to dive headfirst into connecting our newly created application to CouchDB.

# 5
# Connecting your Application to CouchDB

*Now that we have the framework for our application built, let's talk about what needs to happen for our application to communicate with CouchDB.*

We'll talk through the following points in this chapter:

◆ Investigate the quick and easy way to interact with CouchDB, and talk about its shortcomings

◆ Look at existing libraries to ease in PHP and CouchDB development

◆ Install Sag and integrate it into Bones

◆ Have our signup form create CouchDB documents and verify with Futon

## Before we get started

Before we do anything, let's create a database that we'll use from this point forward for Verge. As we've done before, let's create a database using `curl`.

## Time for action – creating a database for Verge with curl

We created a database using `curl` in *Chapter 3, Getting Started with CouchDB and Futon*. Let's quickly recap how to use a `PUT` request to create a new database in CouchDB.

1. Create a new database by running the following command in **Terminal**. Make sure to replace `username` and `password` with the database administrator user that you created in *Chapter 3*.

   ```
   curl -X PUT username:password@localhost:5984/verge
   ```

2. **Terminal** will respond with the following output:

   ```
   {"ok":true}
   ```

## What just happened?

We used **Terminal** to trigger a `PUT` request, using `curl`, to create a database through CouchDB's **RESTful JSON API**. We passed `verge` as the name of the database at the end of CouchDB's root URL. When the database was successfully created, we received a message that everything went okay.

# Diving in head first

In this section, we'll create some quick and dirty code to communicate with CouchDB, and then talk about some of the issues with this approach.

## Adding logic to our signup script

In the previous chapter, we created a form in `views/signup.php`, with the following functionality:

- We asked the user to enter a value for name in a textbox
- We took the value entered in the form and posted it to the signup route
- We used Bones to grab the value passed by the form and set it to a variable called `message` so that we could display it on the home page
- We rendered the home page and displayed the `message` variable

This was a big undertaking on our part, but we weren't able to save anything for later reading or writing.

Let's take this form a few steps further and ask the user to enter both a name and an e-mail address and then save these fields as a document in CouchDB.

## Time for action – adding an e-mail field to the signup form

Let's add an input field so users can enter an e-mail address into the `views/signup.php` page.

1.  Open `signup.php` in your text editor (`/Library/Webserver/Documents/verge/views/signup.php`)

2.  Add the highlighted code to add a label and input field for the e-mail addresses:

    ```
    Signup

    <form action="<?php echo $this->make_route('signup') ?>"
    method="post">
      <label for="name">Name</label>
      <input id="name" name="name" type="text"> <br />
      <label for="email">Email</label>
      <input id="email" name="email" type="text"> <br />
      <input type="Submit" value="Submit">
    </form>
    ```

## What just happened?

We added an additional field to our signup form that will accept the input for an e-mail address. By adding the `email` field to this form, we will be able to access it on form submission and eventually save it as a CouchDB document.

## Using curl calls to post data to CouchDB

We've used `curl` through **Terminal** in previous chapters to interact with CouchDB. You'll be happy to know that you can also use `curl` through PHP. In order to represent the data in CouchDB, we'll first need to get our data into a JSON format.

# Time for action – creating a standard object to encode to JSON

Let's represent a simple object in the form of JSON, so that CouchDB can interpret it.

Open `index.php` in your text editor, and add the following code into the `/signup` POST route:

```php
post('/signup', function($app) {

    $user = new stdClass;
    $user->type = 'user';
    $user->name = $app->form('name');
    $user->email = $app->form('email');

    echo json_encode($user);

    $app->set('message', 'Thanks for Signing Up ' . $app->form('name')
        . '!');

    $app->render('home');

});
```

## What just happened?

We added the code to create an object to store the specifics of a user. We used an instance of `stdClass` and called it `$user`. `stdClass` is PHP's generic empty class, which is useful for anonymous objects, dynamic properties, and hitting the ground running. Because documents require that a type should be set to classify the documents, we are setting this document's type to `user`. We then took the values that were submitted from the form and saved each of them as properties of the `$user` class. Finally, we used a PHP function called `json_encode` to take the object and create a JSON representation of it.

Let's test this out.

1. Open up your browser to `http://localhost/verge/signup`.

2. Enter in John Doe into the **Name** textbox and john@example.com into the **Email** textbox.

3. Click on **Submit**.

4. Your browser will display the following:

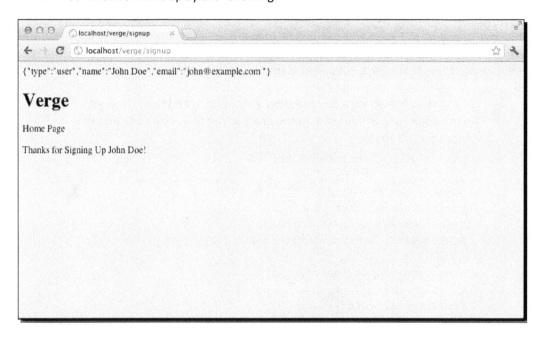

Perfect! Our form was submitted properly, and we were able to represent `stdClass $user` in JSON at the top of our website.

## Committing it to Git

Let's commit our code to Git so that we can look back at this code down the road.

1. Open **Terminal**.

2. Type the following command to change directories to our working directory:

   ```
   cd /Library/Webserver/Documents/verge/
   ```

3. Give Git a description of what we've done since our last commit:

   ```
   git commit -am 'Added functionality to collect name and email
   through stdClass and display it onscreen.'
   ```

Now that we have our data represented in JSON, let's use a `curl` statement to create a CouchDB document using PHP.

## Time for action – creating a CouchDB document with PHP and curl

We've been using `curl` through the command line since the beginning of this book, but this time, we are going to trigger a `curl` statement using PHP.

***1.*** Let's start by initializing a `curl` session, executing it, and then closing it. Open `index.php` in your text editor, and add the following code into the `/signup` POST route:

```
post('/signup', function($app) {

  $user = new stdClass;
  $user->type = 'user';
  $user->name = $app->form('name');
  $user->email = $app->form('email');

  echo json_encode($user);

  $curl = curl_init();

  // curl options

  curl_exec($curl);

  curl_close($curl);

  $app->set('message', 'Thanks for Signing Up ' . $app-
    >form('name') . '!');

  $app->render('home');
});
```

***2.*** Now, let's tell `curl` what to actually execute. We do this with an `options` array. Add the following code between the `curl_init()` and the `curl_exec` statements:

```
post('/signup', function($app) {

  $user = new stdClass;
  $user->name = $app->form('name');
  $user->email = $app->form('email');

  echo json_encode($user);
```

```php
$curl = curl_init();

// curl options

$options = array(
    CURLOPT_URL             => 'localhost:5984/verge',
    CURLOPT_POSTFIELDS      => json_encode($user),
    CURLOPT_HTTPHEADER      => array ("Content-Type:
        application/json"),
    CURLOPT_CUSTOMREQUEST   => 'POST',
    CURLOPT_RETURNTRANSFER  => true,
    CURLOPT_ENCODING        => "utf-8",
    CURLOPT_HEADER          => false,
    CURLOPT_FOLLOWLOCATION  => true,
    CURLOPT_AUTOREFERER     => true
);

curl_setopt_array($curl, $options);

curl_exec($curl);

curl_close($curl);

$app->set('message', 'Thanks for Signing Up ' . $app->
    form('name') . '!');
$app->render('home');
});
```

## What just happened?

We initialized a `curl` session using PHP by first setting a variable `$curl` with the `curl_init()` resource. We then created an array with a variety of keys and values. The reason we picked all of these options isn't too important for us now, but I would like to highlight the first three objects:

1. We are setting the `CURLOPT_URL` option to the URL of the database that we want to save the document into. Remember that this statement will use CouchDB's RESTful JSON API to create a document inside of the `verge` database.

2. We then set `CURLOPT_POSTFIELDS` to the JSON encoded value of our `$user`. This is taking our JSON string and including it as data along with the URL.

3. Finally, we are setting the `CURLOPT_HTTPHEADER` to `array ("Content-Type: application/json")`, so that we can make sure that `curl` knows that we are passing a JSON request.

With our options array set, we need to tell our `curl` instance to use it:

```
curl_setopt_array($curl, $options);
```

We then execute and close `curl` with the following two lines of code:

```
curl_exec($curl);
```

```
curl_close($curl);
```

With this code in our application, we should be able to submit our form and have it posted to CouchDB. Let's test it out.

1. Open your browser to `http://localhost/verge/signup`.

2. Enter `John Doe` into the **Name** textbox and `john@example.com` into the **Email** textbox.

3. Click on **Submit**.

4. Your browser will display the following:

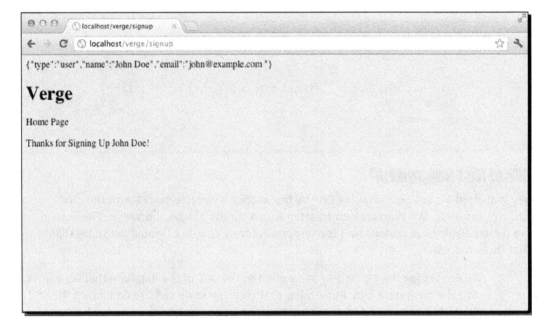

That worked well without any errors, just as before. But this time, a CouchDB document should have been created. Let's check that the document was created properly by using Futon.

1. Open your browser to `http://localhost:5984/_utils/database. html?verge`. This direct link will show you the verge database. You'll see that there's a new document in here! Keep in mind that your `ID` and `rev` will be different from mine:

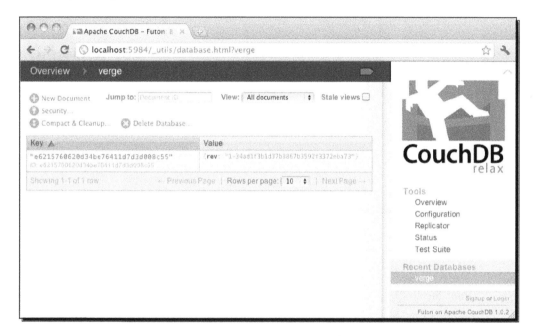

2. Click on the document so that you can see the details.

3.  The data in your document should match up to the information that we passed in using our `curl` session. Notice that `type`, `email`, and `name` were all set properly, and that CouchDB set `_id` and `_rev` for us.

## Committing it to Git

Let's commit our code to Git so that we can refer back to this code in the future.

1.  Open **Terminal**.

2.  Type the following command to change directories to our working directory:

    `cd /Library/Webserver/Documents/verge/`

3.  Give Git a description of what we've done since our last commit:

    `git commit -am 'CouchDB Documents can now be created through the signup form using curl.'`

We just looked at one of the simplest ways to create a CouchDB document with PHP. However, we need to evaluate if the code we just wrote is sustainable and a smart way for us to develop our application.

# Is this technique good enough?

Tough question. Technically, we could build out our application this way, but we would need to add a lot more code and spend the rest of the book refactoring our calls to `curl` until it worked perfectly. Then, we would need to spend a ton of time refactoring our calls into a simple library so that things would be easier to fix. In short, this technique won't work because we want to focus on building our application, instead of sorting out all of the communication issues between PHP and CouchDB. Luckily, there are a variety of CouchDB libraries that we can use to simplify our development process.

# Available CouchDB libraries

There are a variety of libraries that can make our lives easier when developing with PHP and CouchDB. All of the libraries are open source projects, which is great! But, some of these libraries have not been actively worked on to support the newer versions of CouchDB. Therefore, we will need to be selective with the libraries we choose to work with.

A list of some of the PHP and CouchDB libraries can be seen here: `http://wiki.apache. org/couchdb/Getting_started_with_PHP`, and there are a variety of others hosted on GitHub that require a bit more digging.

Each library has strengths, but because simplicity is the key concept of Bones, it makes sense that we should also strive for simplicity in our PHP library. With that being said, our best solution is called **Sag**.

# Sag

Sag is a great PHP library for CouchDB created by Sam Bisbee. Sag's guiding principle is simplicity, creating a powerful interface with little overhead that can be easily integrated with any application structure. It does not force your application to use a framework, special classes for documents, or ORM, but you still can if you want to. Sag accepts the basic PHP data structures (objects, strings, and so on) and returns either raw JSON or the response and the HTTP information in an object.

I'll walk you through installation and the basics of Sag's functionality, but you can also visit Sag's website at: `http://www.saggingcouch.com/` for examples and documentation.

## Downloading and setting up Sag

Sag is pretty unobtrusive and will fit right into our current application structure. All we need to do is use Git to grab Sag from its GitHub repository and place it in our `lib` directory.

## Time for action – using Git to install Sag

Git makes setting up third party libraries really easy and allows us to update to the new versions when they are available.

1. Open **Terminal**.

2. Type the following command to make sure that you are in the working directory:
   ```
   cd /Library/Webserver/Documents/verge/
   ```

3. Add Sag to our repository using Git:
   ```
   git submodule add git://github.com/sbisbee/sag.git lib/sag
   git submodule init
   ```

### What just happened?

We used Git to add Sag into our project using git submodule add, and then we initialized the submodule by typing git submodule init. Git's submodules allow us to have a full-fledged Git repository living inside of our repository. Any time a new release is made to Sag, you can run git submodule update, and you will receive the latest and greatest code.

### Adding Sag to Bones

In order to use Sag, we'll add a few lines into Bones to make sure that our library can see and utilize it.

## Time for action – adding Sag to Bones

Enabling and setting up Sag to work with Bones is extremely easy. Let's walk through it together!

1. Open lib/bones.php inside of our working directory, and add the following line to the top of our class:
   ```php
   <?php

   define('ROOT', __DIR__ . '/..');
   require_once ROOT . '/lib/sag/src/Sag.php';
   ```

**2.** We need to make sure that Sag is ready and available on each request. Let's do this by adding a new variable to Bones called $couch, and setting it in our __construct function:

```
public $route_segments = array();
public $route_variables = array();
public $couch;

public function __construct() {
  $this->route = $this->get_route();
  $this->route_segments = explode('/', trim($this->route, '/'));
  $this->method = $this->get_method();

  $this->couch = new Sag('127.0.0.1', '5984');
  $this->couch->setDatabase('verge');
}
```

## What just happened?

We made sure that Bones could access and use Sag by using require_once to load the Sag resources. We then made sure that each time Bones is constructed, we would define the database server and port and set the database that we want to use.

 Notice that we don't need any credentials to interact with the Verge database because we haven't put any permissions on this database yet.

## Simplifying our code with Sag

With Sag included in our application, we can simplify our database calls, hand off the handling and exception handling to Sag, and focus on building our product.

## Time for action – creating a document with Sag

Now that we have Sag available and ready to use anywhere in our application, let's refactor the saving of the user class that we placed in the /signup post route.

Open index.php, and remove all of the extra code that we added in previous sections so that our /signup post route looks similar to the following code snippet:

```
post('/signup', function($app) {

  $user = new stdClass;
  $user->name = $app->form('name');
```

```
    $user->email = $app->form('email');

    $app->couch->post($user);


    $app->set('message', 'Thanks for Signing Up ' . $app->form('name') .
'!');
    $app->render('home');
});
```

## What just happened?

We used Sag to create a post to our CouchDB database using substantially less code! Sag's post method allows you to pass data with it, so it's really easy to trigger.

Let's quickly go through the signup process again:

1.  Open up your browser to `http://localhost/verge/signup`.
2.  Enter in a new name into the **Name** textbox and a new e-mail into the **Email** textbox.
3.  Click on **Submit**.

A new document was created in CouchDB, so let's check Futon to make sure it's there:

1.  Open your browser to `http://localhost:5984/_utils/database. html?verge`, to look at the verge database.
2.  Click on the second document in the list.
3.  Looking at the details of this new document, you'll see that it has the same structure as the first one that we made.

Perfect! The result ended up exactly as it did with our quick and dirty curl script, but our code is much more simplified, and Sag is handling a lot for us behind the scenes.

> We are currently not catching or handling any errors. We'll talk more about how to handle these in future chapters. Thankfully, CouchDB handles errors in a friendly manner, and Sag has made sure to make it easy to track down problems.

## Adding more structure

It's great that we can create documents so easily, but it's also important that we have a strong structure for our classes, allowing us to stay organized.

# Time for action – including the classes directory

In order for us to use our classes, we'll need to add some code to Bones so that we can automatically load class names as they are used. This will achieve that, so we don't have to continuously include more files as we add new classes.

Add the following code to `lib/bones.php`:

```php
<?php

define('ROOT', __DIR__ . '/..');
require_once ROOT . '/lib/sag/src/Sag.php';

function __autoload($classname) {
    include_once(ROOT . "/classes/" . strtolower($classname) . ".php");
}
```

## What just happened?

We added a __autoload function to our Bones library that will give PHP a last attempt to load a class name if it can't find the class. The __autoload function is passed the $classname, and we use the $classname to find the file of the named class. We are making the requested $classname lowercase using the strtolower function so that we can find the named file. We then added the root of the working directory with the ROOT constant and the classes folder.

## Working with classes

Now that we have the ability to load classes, let's create some! We'll start by creating a base class from which all other classes will inherit properties.

# Time for action – creating a Base object

In this section, we will create a base class called `base.php` that all of our classes will inherit.

1. Let's start by creating a new file called base.php, and placing it in the classes folder inside of the working directory (/Library/Webserver/Documents/verge/ classes/base.php)

2. Create an abstract class with a __construct function in base.php. On __ construct of the object, let's take $type as an option, and set it to a protected variable also called $type.

```php
<?php
abstract class Base
```

```php
{
  protected $type;

  public function __construct($type)
  {
    $this->type = $type;
  }
}
```

3. In order to facilitate the getting and setting of variables in our classes later, let's add the __get() and __set() functions right after the __construct function.

```php
<?php
abstract class Base
{
  protected $type;

  public function __construct($type)
  {
    $this->type = $type;
  }

  public function __get($property) {
    return $this->$property;
  }

  public function __set($property, $value) {
    $this->$property = $value;
  }

}
```

4. Each time we save our object to Couch DB, we'll want to be able to represent it in the JSON string. So, let's create a helper function called to_json() that will convert our object into the JSON format.

```php
<?php
abstract class Base
{
  protected $type;

  public function __construct($type)
  {
    $this->type = $type;
```

```
    }

    public function __get($property) {
      return $this->$property;
    }

    public function __set($property, $value) {
      $this->$property = $value;
    }

    public function to_json() {
      return json_encode(get_object_vars($this));
    }

  }
```

## What just happened?

We created a base class called `base.php` that will serve as the basis for all other classes that we build. Inside the class, we defined a protected variable called `$type`, which will store the classification of the document such as `user` or `post`. Next, we added a `__construct` function that will be called each time the object is created. This function accepts the option `$type`, which we will set in each of the classes that extend on `Base`. We then created the `__get` and `__set` functions. `__get` and `__set` are called **magic methods** and will allow us to use `get` and `set` protected variables without having any extra code. Lastly, we added a function called `to_json` that uses `get_object_vars`, along with `json_encode`, to represent our object in a JSON string. Doing little things like this in our base class will make our lives much easier down the road.

## Time for action – creating a User object

Now that we have our `Base` class created, let's create a `User` class that will house the properties and functions for all things related to users.

1.  Create a new file called `user.php`, and place it in the `classes` folder along with `base.php`.

2.  Let's create a class that extends our `Base` class.
    ```php
    <?php
    class User extends Base
    {

    }
    ```

**3.** Let's add the two properties that we know we need so far: name and email, into our User class.

```php
<?php

class User extends Base
{
  protected $name;
  protected $email;


}
```

**4.** Let's add a __construct function that will tell our Base class that our document type is user on creation.

```php
<?php

class User extends Base
{
  protected $name;
  protected $email;

  public function __construct()
  {
    parent::__construct('user');
  }

}
```

## What just happened?

We created a simple class called user.php that extends Base. **Extends** means that it will inherit the properties and functions that are available so that we can take advantage of them. We then included two protected properties called $name and $email. Finally, we created a __construct function. The construct in this instance tells the parent (which is our Base class) that the type of the document is user.

# Time for action – plugging the User object in

With our new `User` object in our system, we can easily plug it into our application code, and we should be up and running.

1. Open up the `index.php` file, and change `stdClass` to `User()`. While we are at it, we can also remove `$user->type = 'user'` because that's now handled in our class:

```
post('/signup', function($app) {

    $user = new User();
    $user->name = $app->form('name');
    $user->email = $app->form('email');

    $app->couch->post($user);
}
```

2. Adjust the Sag `post` statement so that we can pass our class in the JSON format:

```
post('/signup', function($app) {

    $user = new User();
    $user->name = $app->form('name');
    $user->email = $app->form('email');

    $app->couch->post($user->to_json);
}
```

## What just happened?

We replaced the instance of `stdClass` with `User()`. This will give us complete control over getting and setting the variables. We then removed `$user->type = 'user'` because the `__construct` functions in our `User` and `Base` objects have taken care of that. Finally, we added the `to_json()` function that we created earlier so that we could send our object as a JSON encoded string.

> Sag could technically handle an object by itself with JSON, but it's important that we're able to retrieve a JSON string from our object so that you can interact with CouchDB in any way you want. It's possible that some day in the future you may need to come back and rewrite everything using `curl` or another library. So, it's important that you know how to represent your data in JSON.

# Testing it out

Let's quickly go through our signup process again to make sure that everything is still working:

1.  Open your browser to `http://localhost/verge/signup`.
2.  Enter in a new name into the **Name** textbox and a new e-mail into the **Email** textbox.
3.  Click on **Submit**.

A new document should have been created in CouchDB. Let's check Futon to make sure it's there:

1.  Open up your browser to `http://localhost:5984/_utils/database.html?verge` to look at the verge database.
2.  Click on the third document in the list
3.  Looking at the details of this new document, you'll see that it has the same structure as the first two that we made.

Perfect! Everything worked just as we had it before, but we're now using a more elegant solution that we'll be able to build on top of in future chapters.

# Committing it to Git

Let's commit the code to Git so we've tracked our progress so far:

1.  Open **Terminal**.
2.  Type the following command to change directories to our working directory:

    ```
    cd /Library/Webserver/Documents/verge/
    ```

3.  We've added some new files in our `classes` folder. So, let's make sure we add those files to Git.

    ```
    git add classes/*
    ```

4.  Give Git a description of what we've done since our last commit:

    ```
    git commit -am 'Added class structure for Users and tested its
    functionality'
    ```

By using the `classes/*` syntax, we are telling Git to add every file inside of the classes folder. This is handy when you've added multiple files and don't want to add each file individually.

# Wrapping up

We've completed the code for this chapter. It's always good practice to push your code to GitHub once in a while. In fact, when you are working with multiple developers, it's crucial. I won't remind you to do this any more in this book. So, make sure you do it often:

```
git push origin master
```

This line of code reads like a sentence if you add just a few words in between. The sentence is telling Git to `push` to the `origin` (which we have defined as GitHub), and we want to send the `master` branch.

# Summary

I hope you enjoyed this chapter. It's fun when all of these technologies work together and allow us to easily save things to CouchDB.

Let's recap what we talked about in this chapter:

- ◆ We looked at several different ways we could talk to CouchDB with PHP
- ◆ We tied Sag into Bones
- ◆ We built an object-oriented class structure that will save us a lot of headaches down the road
- ◆ We tested to make sure that when we submitted our signup form, a CouchDB document was created

In the next chapter, we are going to actively look at some of the great functionality that CouchDB already has plugged in for our users and how we can use CouchDB to build out the standard signup and login processes that most applications have. Stretch your typing fingers, and get yourself a nice, big cup of coffee as we're about to have some real fun.

# 6

# Modeling Users

*Believe it or not, we've already done quite a bit to make our interactions with CouchDB a simple process. In this chapter, we'll get right into the meat of CouchDB and start to model our user documents.*

To be more specific we will:

◆ Install Bootstrap, a toolkit from Twitter that will handle the heavy lifting of CSS, forms, buttons, and more

◆ Take a close look at how CouchDB stores user documents by default and how we can add fields to them

◆ Add basic functionality for users so they can sign up, log in, and log out of our application

◆ Learn how to handle exceptions and errors

This is going to be our most rewarding chapter yet; you'll love offloading some of the standard authentication and security to CouchDB. Buckle up. It's going to be a fun ride!

## Before we get started

We've played around with a lot of files to test Bones and Sag, but you'll notice that our application is still looking pretty barren. So, let's spruce up the design a bit. Since designing and implementing UIs isn't the purpose of this book, we'll use a toolkit called **Bootstrap** to do the heavy lifting for us. Bootstrap (http://twitter.github.com/bootstrap/) was created by Twitter to kickstart the development of web applications and sites. It will allow us to breeze past front-end development without too much work. Let's get Bootstrap up and running and then do some housekeeping on our layout.

# Cleaning up our interface by installing Bootstrap

Setting up Bootstrap is incredibly easy. We could reference the CSS on their remote servers, but we'll download and call the CSS locally since it's best practice to reduce the amount of external calls.

## Time for action – installing Bootstrap locally

Installing Bootstrap is a breeze; we'll cover the basics of getting it installed in this section.

*1.* Open your browser, and go to `http://twitter.github.com/bootstrap/`.

*2.* Click on **Download Bootstrap**.

*3.* A `.zip` file will be downloaded into your `downloads` folder; unzip it by double-clicking on it or by using your favorite unzip tool.

*4.* You will find three directories inside the `bootstrap` folder, namely `css`, `img`, and `js`, each containing a number of files.

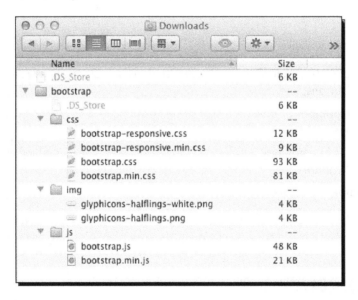

**5.** Copy all of the files in each of these folders into the respective folders in your `verge` project: `/public/css`, `public/img`, and `public/js`. Your `verge` directory should look similar to the following screenshot when you're done:

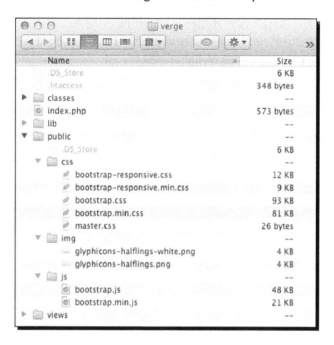

## What just happened?

We just installed Twitter's Bootstrap into our project by downloading a `.zip` file containing all of the assets and by placing them in the correct folders on our local machine.

Just by looking at the new files that we have in our project, you might notice that each file appears to show up twice, one with `min` inside of the filename and one without. These two files are identical, except for the fact that the one that contains `min` in the file name has been minified. **Minified** means that all of the non-essential characters are removed from the code to decrease the file size. The removed characters include things such as white-spaces, new-line characters, comments, and much more. Because these files are loaded on demand from the website, it's important that they are as small as possible to speed your application up. If you tried to open a minified file, it's usually pretty hard to tell what's going on, which is fine because we don't want to make any changes in these files to begin with.

It might be clear what all of these files do—the css files are defining some of the global styles of Bootstrap. The img files are used to help us use icons around our site if we want to, and the js files are used to help us add interaction, transitions, and effects to our site. But, inside of the css folder, there are both bootstrap and bootstrap-responsive css files, which can be confusing. **Responsive design** is something that has really exploded over the past few years, and in itself, has many books written about it. In short bootstrap includes styles in the bootstrap-responsive file to help our site work on different resolutions and devices. Out of the box, our website therefore should work on both web and modern mobile devices (for the most part).

Now, you can probably tell why I chose to use Bootstrap; we just gained a whole lot of functionality just by copying files into our project. But, everything isn't hooked up quite yet; we need to tell our layout.php file where to look so that it can use these new files.

## Time for action – including Bootstrap and adjusting our layout to work with it

Because the Bootstrap framework is just a series of files, it'll be a breeze for us to include it in our project, just as we did with our master.css file in *Chapter 4, Starting your Application*.

*1.* Start by adding a link to bootstrap.min.css and bootstrap-responsive. min.css before master.css in the layout.php file:

```
<head>

<link href="<?php echo $this->make_route('/css/bootstrap.min.css')
    ?>" rel="stylesheet" type="text/css" />

<link href="<?php echo $this->make_route('/css/master.css') ?>"
    rel="stylesheet" type="text/css" />

<link href="<?php echo $this->make_route('/css/bootstrap-
responsive.min.css') ?>" rel="stylesheet" type="text/css" />
</head>
```

*2.* Next, let's make sure that Bootstrap works well in older versions of Internet Explorer and mobile browsers by adding the following little bit of code:

```
<link href="<?php echo $this->make_route('/css/bootstrap-
    responsive.min.css') ?>" rel="stylesheet" type="text/css" />

<!--[if lt IE 9]>
<script src="http://html5shim.googlecode.com/svn/trunk/html5.js">
</script>
<![endif]-->
<meta name="viewport" content="width=device-width,
initial-scale=1.0">

</head>
```

**3.** Let's make a clean and simple wrapper for our application by replacing the contents of the `views/layout.php` file with the following:

```
<body>
  <div class="navbar navbar-fixed-top">
    <div class="navbar-inner">
      <div class="container">
        <a class="btn btn-navbar" data-toggle="collapse" data-
          target=".nav-collapse">
          <span class="icon-bar"></span>
          <span class="icon-bar"></span>
          <span class="icon-bar"></span>
        </a>
        <a class="brand" href="<?php echo $this->make_route('/')
          ?>">Verge</a>
        <div class="nav-collapse">
          <ul class="nav">
            <li><a href="<?php echo $this->make_route('/') ?>">
              Home
            </a></li>
            <li>
              <a href="<?php echo $this->make_route('/signup')
                ?>">Signup</a>
            </li>
          </ul>
        </div>
      </div>
    </div>
  </div>

  <div class="container">
    <?php include($this->content); ?>
  </div>
</body>
```

**4.** Remove the contents of the `master.css` file, and replace them with the following to make a few small adjustments to our layout:

```
.page-header {margin-top: 50px;}
input {height: 20px;}
```

## What just happened?

We included Bootstrap in our `layout.php` file and made sure that the versions of Internet Explorer would work okay by adding an HTML5 shim that a lot of developers use. If you want to find out more about how this works, feel free to visit `http://html5shim.googlecode.com/`.

Next, we added some HTML to conform to the CSS definitions defined in Bootstrap. It's not too important for you to understand why the HTML is set up like it is, but if you're curious, you can refer to the main page of Bootstrap to learn more (`http://twitter.github.com/bootstrap/`). We then added a few rules to our `main.css` file that added additional styles on top of Bootstrap. I did this to create a little bit of space in our application, so things weren't cluttered.

If you were to go to the home page now by going to `http://localhost/verge/`, the header definitely looks cool, but the home page needs some love. Let's quickly clean up the home page.

## Time for action – sprucing up the home page

Bootstrap is going to save us some real time again; we just need a little bit of HTML markup for our application to look pretty nice! Replace the contents of `views/home.php` with the following:

```
<div class="hero-unit">
  <h1>Welcome to Verge!</h1>
  <p>Verge is a simple social network that will make you popular.</p>
  <p>
    <a href="<?php echo $this->make_route('/signup') ?>" class="btn
      btn-primary btn-large">
      Signup Now
    </a>
  </p>
</div>
```

## What just happened?

We just added a nice clean layout for our home page with a button to prompt people to sign up when they come to our site. Notice that we removed `<? php echo $message; ?>` from the file, when we originally added that to display simple messages to our users, but we're going to explore a cleaner way of doing that later in this chapter.

Ready to see some magic? Open your browser, and go to `http://localhost/verge/`.

We've barely had to spend any time on the design, but we already have a much friendlier application. This new design is going to come in handy later, when we get deeper into handling users.

Ready to see something cool? Try making your browser window smaller, and see what happens.

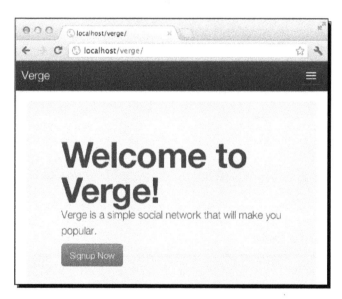

Notice how the content adjusts to the screen size; this means that on a mobile device, your application will adjust so that it's easy to view. Bootstrap's responsive boilerplate code is just the beginning. You could choose to show and hide content, depending on the size of the browser.

With the browser window smaller, you'll notice that the navigation bar has also been condensed, and instead of seeing your links, you see a button with three bars on it. Try clicking on it...nothing happens!

This component requires Bootstrap's JavaScript file, as well as a JavaScript library called **jQuery**. It's not crucial for us to have this all working yet, so let's come back to it in the next chapter!

## Moving all user files into the user folder

Our application is going to start growing quite a bit in this section. Our views are going to get pretty messy if we keep throwing our files around as we currently are. Let's perform a little housekeeping and add some structure to our `views` directory.

## Time for action – organizing our user views

As we continue to create views for our application, it will be smart for us to have some organization to make sure that we keep things nice and straightforward.

*1.* Create a folder called `user` inside the `views` directory.

*2.* Move the existing `signup.php` view into this folder. The resulting directory structure will look similar to the following screenshot:

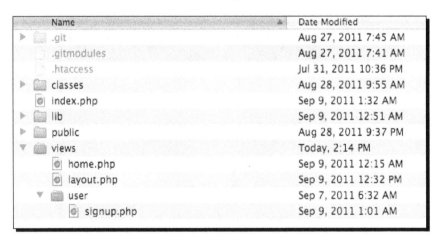

*3.* We need to update `index.php` and let it know where to find the signup view that we just moved:

```
get('/signup', function($app) {
  $app->render('user/signup');
});
```

## *What just happened?*

We cleaned up our `views` folder structure by creating a `user` folder, into which we will put all of the views that relate to users. We then moved our existing `signup.php` file into the `user` folder and told our `index.php` file where to find the `user/signup.php` file. Notice that the route for the signup page, `/signup`, hasn't changed at all.

# Designing our user documents

We've seen in *Chapter 3*, *Getting Started with CouchDB and Futon*, how CouchDB looks at user documents. In this chapter, we are going to learn how to leverage existing CouchDB functionality and add some additional fields on top of it.

## How CouchDB looks at basic user documents

CouchDB already has a mechanism for storing user documents, which we've already seen and used. We are going to use this same structure for the users of our application:

```
{
    "_id": "org.couchdb.user:your_username",
    "_rev": "1-b9af54a7cdc392c2c298591f0dcd81f3",
    "name": "your_username",
    "password_sha": "3bc7d6d86da61fed6d4d82e1e4d1c3ca587aecc8",
    "roles": [],
    "salt": "9812acc4866acdec35c903f0cc072c1d",
    "type": "user"
}
```

These seven fields are required by CouchDB for users to operate correctly in CouchDB:

- `_id` is the unique identifier of the user. It needs to start with `org.couchdb.user:` and end with the same value of the `name` attribute. These roles are enforced by the `_auth` design document. We haven't talked too much about design documents yet. But, at this point, it's good for you to know that design documents are code that run directly inside the database. They can be used to enforce validation and business roles.

- `_rev` is the revision identifier of the document. We quickly touched on revisions in *Chapter 3*.

- `name` is the username of the user. This field is required by the `_auth` design document, and it also needs to match the value of the `_id` of the document after the `:` character.

- `password_sha` is the SHA-1 encrypted value of the password after it has been combined with the `salt`. We'll cover SHA-1 encryption in just a bit.

- ◆ `roles` is an array of privileges that a user might have. By having a value of `[]`, we know that this user has no special privileges.

- ◆ `salt` is the unique `salt` of the user. The `salt` is combined with the plaintext value of the password and is passed through SHA-1 encryption to result in the value of `password_sha`.

- ◆ `type` is the identifier that CouchDB uses to identify the document type. Remember that CouchDB is a flat document store. This `type` field identifies the classification of a document.

These user documents are unique in that they have a small amount of structure that is required, but we can always add additional fields to these. Let's do that next!

# Adding more fields to the user document

Let's talk about a few extra fields that we know we'll want to collect information from the users of Verge. Keep in mind that you can always add more fields if your application needs it.

- ◆ **Username**: We know that we'll want to be able to store a unique username, so that our users will have a unique URL, such as `/user/johndoe`. Luckily, this functionality is already handled by CouchDB's `name` field. With that in mind, there's nothing to do here. We'll just use the existing `name` instead!

- ◆ **Full name**: The full name of the user, so we can display the name of the user as `John Doe`. This will be a user-friendly name that we can use to display to visiting users, we'll need to add a field to the documents to support this.

- ◆ **E-mail**: An e-mail address, so that we can communicate with the user, such as for notification e-mails: `john@example.com`. We're actually already saving the e-mails in our current class, so we can ignore this as well.

Sounds easy enough; we just need to add one field! Any time you add new fields to a document, you should think about how you need to format it. Let's talk about the different approaches that we could take with CouchDB.

## Discussing options for adding these fields

There are a variety of ways that we might use to add fields on top of CouchDB's basic user documents:

- ◆ We could create a new type of document and call it `verge_user`. This document would contain any additional user attributes that we need in our application and then would have a reference back to the user document.

- ◆ We could create an array inside our user document with the application-specific attributes and add all of our user attributes there.

- ◆ Or we could just add the two new fields inside our user documents.

I think, for now, we can all agree that by adding one field, we can just go with the last option mentioned.

With that in mind, our final document will look similar to the following:

```
{
    "_id": "org.couchdb.user:johndoe",
    "_rev": "1-b9af54a7cdc392c2c298591f0dcd81f3",
    "name": "johndoe",
    "full_name": "John Doe",
    "email": "john@example.com",
    "password_sha": "3bc7d6d86da61fed6d4d82e1e4d1c3ca587aecc8",
    "roles": [],
    "salt": "9812acc4866acdec35c903f0cc072c1d",
    "type": "user"
}
```

It might be strange for you to see variations of the user's name in so many places: _id, name, and full_name. But remember that CouchDB has a good reason for doing this. By storing the username in the _id, CouchDB will automatically check to make sure that each username is unique.

> Keep in mind that we might want to get more creative if we want to start storing fields such as website, biography, or location. We'll talk more about this later on in the book.

## Adding support for the additional fields

In order for us to add these fields to our user documents, we don't have to change much in our code; we just need to add a few more variables into our user.php class.

## Time for action – adding the fields to support the user documents

We already have the basic structure of user documents set up in the classes/user.php file, but let's go through and add a few more fields.

**1.** We currently aren't setting _id in any of our projects, but we'll need to do that for our user documents. Let's open up classes/base.php, and add _id so that we have the option of setting _id on any document.

```php
<?php

abstract class Base {
        protected $_id;
        protected $type;
```

**2.** We need to add all of the user fields that we just discussed into the `classes/user.php` file, and a few others. Add the following code to `classes/user.php` so that it looks as follows:

```php
<?php

class User extends Base {
        protected $name;
        protected $email;
        protected $full_name;
        protected $salt;
        protected $password_sha;
        protected $roles;
```

## What just happened?

We added all the fields that we'll need to be able to save user documents into our system. We added `_id` to the `base.php` class, because we know that every CouchDB document requires this field. We have been able to live without `_id` because CouchDB has automatically set one for us so far. However, in this chapter, we'll need to be able to set and retrieve `_id` for our user documents. We then added `full_name` and a few other fields that might throw you off a bit. `$salt` and `$password_sha` are used to safely store passwords. This process is easier to explain with an example, so we'll go over this in detail in our signup process. Lastly, we added roles, which will be empty in this book but can be useful for you to develop a role-based system, allowing certain users to be able to see certain parts of your application, and so on.

Now that we have the user structure defined, we need to walk through the signup process, which is a bit more complex than the CouchDB document creation we've done so far.

# The signup process

Now that we have support for all of the fields in the user class, let's add support for users to sign up for Verge. Signing up is a bit of a complicated process, but we'll try to break it down by going step-by-step. In this section we will:

1. Define our database admin user and password so that we can create new user documents

2. Create a new signup interface to support all the fields we've added

3. Add a Bootstrap helper to make creating form inputs much easier

4. Develop a quick and dirty implementation of the signup process

5. Dig deeper into using SHA-1 encryption for our passwords

6. Refactor our signup process so that it is a bit more structured

# A little administrator setup

In *Chapter 3*, we locked down `our _users` database, so we could secure our user data, meaning that any time we deal with the `_users` database, we need to provide the administrator login. For this, we'll add PHP constants for the user and the password at the top of the `index.php` file, so that we can reference it any time we need to perform an administrator function. Don't worry if this seems messy; we'll clean this up later in the book.

```php
<?php
include 'lib/bones.php';

define('ADMIN_USER', 'tim');
define('ADMIN_PASSWORD', 'test');
```

# Updating the interface

If you were to open your browser and look at the signup page now by going to: `http://localhost/verge/signup`, you'd notice that it's out of date with our new Bootstrap changes. In fact, you probably can't even see all of the input boxes! Let's use Bootstrap to help clean up our signup interface so that it looks correct.

1. Replace all of the contents of the `views/user/signup.php` page with the following HTML code:

```html
<div class="page-header">
  <h1>Signup</h1>
</div>

<div class="row">
  <div class="span12">
    <form class="form-vertical" action="<?php echo $this-
      >make_route('/signup') ?>" method="post">
      <fieldset>
        <label for="full_name">Full Name</label>
        <input class="input-large" id="full_name" name="full_name"
          type="text" value="">
        <label for="email">Email</label>
        <input class="input-large" id="email" name="email"
          type="text" value="">
        <div class="form-actions">
          <button class="btn btn-primary">Sign Up!</button>
        </div>
      </fieldset>
    </form>
  </div>
</div>
```

2. Refresh the signup page, and you'll see our awesome form now!

Our form looks nice and clean. But, let's be honest, adding the code for the input fields will start to become a pain as we add more fields. Let's create a little helper class to help us create an HTML markup that can play nicely with Bootstrap:

3. Create a new file in the `lib` directory called `bootstrap.php`.

4. Make a reference to `lib/bootstrap.php` in `bones.php`.

```php
define('ROOT', __DIR__ . '/..');

require_once ROOT . '/lib/bootstrap.php';
require_once ROOT . '/lib/sag/src/Sag.php';
```

5. Open up `lib/bootstrap.php`, and create a basic class.

```php
<?php

    class Bootstrap {

    }
```

6. We're going to create a function called `make_input` that will accept four arguments: `$id`, `$label`, `$type`, and `$value`.

```php
<?php

    class Bootstrap {

        public static function make_input($id, $label, $type, $value =
        '') {
```

```
        echo '<label for="' . $id . '">' . $label . '</label>
           <input class="input-large" id="' . $id . '" name="' . $id
           . '" type="' . $type . '" value="' . $value . '">';
    }

  }
```

7. Go back to `views/user/signup.php`, and simplify the code to use the new `make_input` function.

```
<div class="page-header">
  <h1>Signup</h1>
</div>

<div class="row">
  <div class="span12">
    <form action="<?php echo $this->make_route('/signup') ?>"
      method="post">
      <fieldset>
        <?php Bootstrap::make_input('full_name', 'Full Name',
          'text'); ?>
        <?php Bootstrap::make_input('email', 'Email', 'text'); ?>

        <div class="form-actions">
          <button class="btn btn-primary">Sign Up!</button>
        </div>
      </fieldset>
    </form>
  </div>
</div>
```

8. Now that we have `lib/bootstrap.php` to make our life easier, let's ask our users for two more fields: `username` and `password`.

```
<fieldset>
  <?php Bootstrap::make_input('full_name', 'Full Name', 'text');
    ?>
  <?php Bootstrap::make_input('email', 'Email', 'text'); ?>
  <?php Bootstrap::make_input('username', 'Username', 'text'); ?>
  <?php Bootstrap::make_input('password', 'Password', 'password');
    ?>

  <div class="form-actions">
    <button class="btn btn-primary">Sign Up!</button>
  </div>
</fieldset>
```

9. Refresh your browser, and you'll see a dramatically improved signup form. If it doesn't look like the following screenshot, check to make sure your code matches mine.

Our form looks great! Unfortunately, it doesn't actually sign up a user yet when you click on **Sign Up!**. Let's change that in this next section.

## Quick and dirty signup

For now, we will write the user signup code directly into `index.php`. We'll refactor this code a few times, and by the end of the chapter, we will move the bulk of the signup functionality into the `classes/user.php` file.

## Time for action – handling simple user signup

Let's go through the signup process step-by-step, in which we'll rebuild the code in our signup `POST` route from scratch. I'll explain each piece of code on the way, and then, we will do a full recap at the end of this section.

1. Open `index.php`, and start by collecting the simple fields: `full_name`, `email`, and `roles`. The fields `full_name` and `email` will come directly from the form submission, and `roles` we will set to an empty array because this user has no special permissions.

```
post('/signup', function($app) {
    $user = new User();
```

```
     $user->full_name = $app->form('full_name');
     $user->email = $app->form('email');
     $user->roles = array();
```

**2.** Next, we'll want to capture the username that the user submitted, but we'll want to safeguard against weird characters or spaces, so we'll use a regular expression to convert the posted username to a lowercase string without any special characters. The end result will serve as our `name` field and also as a part of the ID. Remember that user documents require that `_id` starts with `org.couchdb.user` and ends with the `name` of the user.

```
post('/signup', function($app) {
     $user = new User();
     $user->full_name = $app->form('full_name');
     $user->email = $app->form('email');
     $user->roles = array();
     $user->name = preg_replace('/[^a-z0-9-]/', '',
strtolower($app-
     >form('username')));
     $user->_id = 'org.couchdb.user:' . $user->name;
```

**3.** In order to encrypt the plain-text value of the password that the user entered, we'll temporarily set a string as the value of `salt`. We'll then pass the plain-text password into a SHA-1 function, and save it in `password_sha`. We'll go deeper into how SHA-1 works in just a few moments.

```
post('/signup', function($app) {
     $user = new User();
     $user->full_name = $app->form('full_name');
     $user->email = $app->form('email');
     $user->roles = array();
     $user->name = preg_replace('/[^a-z0-9-]/', '',
strtolower($app-
     >form('username')));
     $user->_id = 'org.couchdb.user:' . $user->name;
     $user->salt = 'secret_salt';
     $user->password_sha = sha1($app->form('password') . $user-
     >salt);
```

**4.** In order to save the user document, we need to set the database to `_users`, and log in as the admin user that we set with our PHP constants. Then, we will put the user to CouchDB using Sag.

```
post('/signup', function($app) {
     $user = new User();
     $user->full_name = $app->form('full_name');
     $user->email = $app->form('email');
     $user->roles = array();
```

```
        $user->name = preg_replace('/[^a-z0-9-]/', '',
strtolower($app-
    >form('username')));
        $user->_id = 'org.couchdb.user:' . $user->name;
        $user->salt = 'secret_salt';
        $user->password_sha = sha1($app->form('password') . $user-
    >salt);
        $app->couch->setDatabase('_users');
        $app->couch->login(ADMIN_USER, ADMIN_PASSWORD);
        $app->couch->put($user->_id, $user->to_json());
```

**5.** Finally, let's close the user signup function and render the home page.

```
post('/signup', function($app) {
        $user = new User();
        $user->full_name = $app->form('full_name');
        $user->email = $app->form('email');
        $user->roles = array();
        $user->name = preg_replace('/[^a-z0-9-]/', '',
strtolower($app-
    >form('username')));
        $user->_id = 'org.couchdb.user:' . $user->name;
        $user->salt = 'secret_salt';
        $user->password_sha = sha1($app->form('password') . $user-
    >salt);
        $app->couch->setDatabase('_users');
        $app->couch->login(ADMIN_USER, ADMIN_PASSWORD);
        $app->couch->put($user->_id, $user->to_json());
        $app->render('home');
});
```

## What just happened?

We just added code to set all of the values for our CouchDB user documents. Collecting the values of full_name, email, and roles was pretty straightforward; we just performed a simple call to grab the values from the posted form. Setting name got more complex with us transforming the posted value of username to a lowercase string, from which we used a **Regular Expression (Regex)** function to change any special characters to blank characters. With a clean name, we appended it to org.couchdb.user and saved it to the document's _id. Whew! That was a mouthful.

Stepping quickly into the world of encryption, we set a static (and very unsafe) `salt`. Combining the `salt`, along with the plain-text password in a SHA-1 function, resulted in an encrypted password that was saved to our object's `password_sha` field. Next, we set the database of Sag by using `setDatabase`, so that we could talk to CouchDB's `_users` database. In order for us to communicate with the users, we needed to have administrator credentials. So, we used the `ADMIN_USER` and `ADMIN_PASSWORD` constants to log in to CouchDB. Finally, we used the HTTP verb `PUT` to create the document in CouchDB and rendered the home page for the user.

Let's test this all out and see what happens when we submit the signup form.

1. Open up the signup page by going to `http://localhost/verge/signup` in your browser.

2. Fill in the form, with **Full Name** set as `John Doe`, **Email** set as `john@example.com`, **Username** set as `johndoe`, and **Password** set as `temp123`. When you're finished, click on **Sign Up!**

3. Your user has been created! Let's go to Futon by going to `http://localhost:5984/_utils`, and look at the `_users` database for the new document.

4. Perfect, everything should have saved correctly! When you are finished looking at this, delete the user by clicking on **Delete Document**. If you are not currently logged in as an admin user, you'll need to log in first before CouchDB will allow you to delete the document.

   I had you delete the user because our password might as well be in plain-text if every user has a `salt` equal to `secret_salt`. In order for you to understand why this is so, let's take a step back and look at what SHA-1 does.

# SHA-1

Storing plain-text passwords is one of the biggest no-no's when it comes to security. Because of that, we are using SHA-1 (`http://en.wikipedia.org/wiki/SHA-1`) to create a cryptographic hash. SHA-1 is a cryptographic hash function created by the **National Security Agency (NSA)**. The basic principle behind SHA-1 is that we combine a password with a **salt** to make our password indistinguishable. **Salt** is a string of random bits that we combine with our password to make our password encrypted in a unique fashion.

In the signup code we just wrote, we skipped over something pretty important. Our `salt` was being set to `secret_salt` every time. What we really need to do is create a random `salt` for each password.

In order to create the random salt, we can use CouchDB's RESTful JSON API. Couch provides a resource at `http://localhost:5984/_uuids` that, when called, will return a unique `UUID` for us to use. Each `UUID` is a long and random string, which is exactly what a salt needs! Sag makes getting a UUID super easy with the help of a function called `generateIDs`.

Let's update our signup code to reflect what we just talked about. Open `index.php`, and change the setting of the `salt` value to match the following:

```
post('/signup', function($app) {
    $user = new User();
    $user->full_name = $app->form('full_name');
    $user->email = $app->form('email');
    $user->roles = array();
    $user->name = preg_replace('/[^a-z0-9-]/', '', strtolower($app-
     >form('username')));
    $user->_id = 'org.couchdb.user:' . $user->name;
        $user->salt = $app->couch->generateIDs(1)->body->uuids[0];
    $user->password_sha = sha1($app->form('password') . $user->salt);
    $app->couch->setDatabase('_users');
    $app->couch->login(ADMIN_USER, ADMIN_PASSWORD);
    $app->couch->put($user->_id, $user->to_json());
    $app->render('home');
});
```

## Testing the signup process again

Now that we've fixed the insecurities of our salt, let's go back and try the signup process again.

1.  Open up the signup page by going to `http://localhost/verge/signup` in your browser.

2.  Fill in the form, with **Full Name** being `John Doe`, **Email** being `john@example.com`, **Username** being `johndoe`, and **Password** being `temp123`. When you're finished, click on **Sign Up!**.

3. Your user has been created! Let's go to Futon by going to
   `http://localhost:5984/_utils`, and look for our new document
   in the _users database. This time our `salt` is random and unique!

# Refactoring the signup process

As I mentioned earlier, we are going to refactor this code into clean functions inside our user class, instead of it sitting directly in `index.php`. We want to reserve using `index.php` for handling routes, passing values, and rendering views.

## Time for action – cleaning up the signup process

Let's clean up our signup code by creating a public function, called `signup`, inside the `User` class.

1. Open `classes/user.php`, and create a `public` function for signup.

   ```php
   public function signup($username,$password) {


   }
   ```

**2.** Enter the code to match the code below. It's almost identical to the code that
we entered in the last section, except that instead of referencing $user, we are
referencing $this. You'll also notice that full_name and email aren't located in
this function; you'll see them in just a second.

```
public function signup($username, $password) {
        $bones = new Bones();
        $bones->couch->setDatabase('_users');
        $bones->couch->login(ADMIN_USER, ADMIN_PASSWORD);

        $this->roles = array();
        $this->name = preg_replace('/[^a-z0-9-]/', '',
strtolower($username));
        $this->_id = 'org.couchdb.user:' . $this->name;
        $this->salt = $bones->couch->generateIDs(1)->body->uuids[0];
        $this->password_sha = sha1($password . $this->salt);

        $bones->couch->put($this->_id, $this->to_json());
}
```

**3.** Open up index.php, and clean up the signup route so that it matches the
following code:

```
post('/signup', function($app) {
        $user = new User();
        $user->full_name = $app->form('full_name');
        $user->email = $app->form('email');
        $user->signup($app->form('username'), $app-
>form('password'));

        $app->set('message', 'Thanks for Signing Up ' . $user->full_
name
        . '!');
        $app->render('home');
});
```

## *What just happened?*

We created a public function, called `signup`, that will house all of the signup code needed for our users to sign up. We then copied much of the code from the `index.php` signup route. You'll notice that there are some new things in there that we didn't see before. For instance, all references to `$user` have been changed to `$this`, because all of the variables we are using are attached to the current user object. You'll also notice that, at the beginning, we created a new `Bones` object so that we could use it. We also created Sag, which we've connected to Bones, which we were able to initialize without causing any overheard, because we are using the singleton pattern. Remember that the singleton pattern allows us to call the same object that we are using elsewhere on this request without creating a new one. Finally, we went back to the `index.php` file and simplified our signup code route so that we are only dealing with values that are coming directly from the forms. We then passed the untouched username and password through the signup function, so we could process them and execute the signup code.

Our signup code is now clean and operating on the class level and out of our application's hair. But, if you were to test our form a bit, you would realize that it's not foolproof yet.

## Exception handling and resolving errors

If you were to try to go back to your signup form and save another document with the name `John Doe`, you would see a pretty unfriendly error page that looks something similar to the following screenshot:

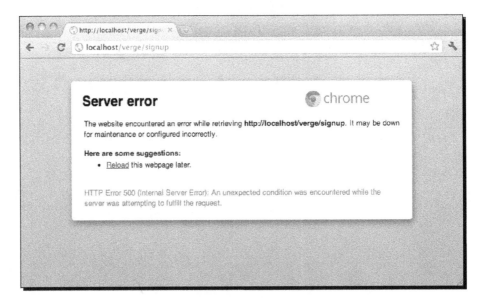

If you are using a browser other than Chrome, you probably received a different message, but the result is still the same. Something bad happened that we didn't expect, and even worse, we aren't capturing these exceptions.

What happens when something goes wrong? How will we figure out what broke? The answer is: we look at the logs.

# Deciphering error logs

When PHP and Apache are working together, they produce a lot of logs for us to look at. Some are access-level logs, and others are error-level. So let's see if we can investigate what's happening here by looking at the Apache error log.

## Time for action – examining Apache's log

Let's start by finding Apache's error log.

1. Open Terminal.

2. Run the following command to ask Apache's `config` file where it's saving the logs to:

   ```
   grep ErrorLog /etc/apache2/httpd.conf
   ```

3. Terminal will return something similar to the following:

   ```
   # ErrorLog: The location of the error log file.
   # If you do not specify an ErrorLog directive within a
   <VirtualHost>
   ErrorLog "/private/var/log/apache2/error_log"
   ```

4. Retrieve the last few lines of the log by running the following command:

   ```
   tail /private/var/log/apache2/error_log
   ```

5. The log will show you a bunch of things, but the most important message is this one, that says PHP `Fatal error`. Yours might be slightly different, but the overall message is the same.

   ```
   [Sun Sep 11 22:10:31 2011] [error] [client 127.0.0.1] PHP Fatal
   error:  Uncaught exception 'SagCouchException' with message
   'CouchDB Error: conflict (Document update conflict.)' in /
   Library/WebServer/Documents/verge/lib/sag/src/Sag.php:1126\
   nStack trace:\n#0 /Library/WebServer/Documents/verge/lib/
   sag/src/Sag.php(286): Sag->procPacket('PUT', '/_users/org.
   cou...', '{"name":"johndoe')\n#1 /Library/WebServer/Documents/
   verge/classes/user.php(30): Sag->put('org.couchdb.use...',
   ```

```
'{"name":"johndoe')\n#2 /Library/WebServer/Documents/verge/
index.php(20): User->signup('w')\n#3 /Library/WebServer/
Documents/verge/lib/bones.php(91): {closure}(Object(Bones))\n#4
/Library/WebServer/Documents/verge/lib/bones.php(17):
Bones::register('/signup', Object(Closure), 'POST')\n#5 /
Library/WebServer/Documents/verge/index.php(24): post('/signup',
Object(Closure))\n#6 {main}\n  thrown in /Library/WebServer/
Documents/verge/lib/sag/src/Sag.php on line 1126, referer: http://
localhost/verge/signup
```

## What just happened?

We asked Apache where it was storing the logs, once we found out where the log file was being saved. We used a `tail` command to return the last few lines of the Apache log.

> There are a variety of ways to read logs that we won't go deep into, but do what makes you feel comfortable. You can research more on `tail` by searching the Internet, or you can open logs in the console application that comes pre-installed on your Mac OSX machine.

Looking at the PHP Fatal error that we received is pretty confusing. If you start looking deeper into this, you'll see that it's a CouchDB error. To be more specific, the main line in this error is:

```
Uncaught exception 'SagCouchException' with message 'CouchDB Error:
conflict (Document update conflict.)
```

This message means that CouchDB isn't happy with what we are passing to it, and we aren't handling the exception that Sag is throwing to us in the form of `SagCouchException`. `SagCouchException` is a class that will help us decipher exceptions thrown by CouchDB, but in order to do that, we'll need to know what status code is being passed back by CouchDB.

In order to get the status code, we'll need to look at our CouchDB logs.

## Time for action: Examine CouchDB's log

Since we all installed CouchDB the same way with Homebrew, we can be sure that our CouchDB logs all live in the same location. With that in mind, let's look at our CouchDB log.

1. Open Terminal.

2. Retrieve the last few lines of the log by running the following command:
   ```
   tail /usr/local/var/log/couchdb/couch.log
   ```

**3.** Terminal will return something similar to the following:

```
[Mon, 12 Sep 2011 16:04:56 GMT] [info] [<0.879.0>] 127.0.0.1 - -
'GET' /_uuids?count=1 200


[Mon, 12 Sep 2011 16:04:56 GMT] [info] [<0.879.0>] 127.0.0.1 - -
'PUT' /_users/org.couchdb.user:johndoe 409
```

## What just happened?

We used a `tail` command to return the last few lines of the CouchDB log.

The first record you'll notice is `/uuids?count=1`, which is us grabbing the UUIDs for `salt` in our `signup` function. Notice that it returned a `200` status, which means that it executed successfully.

The next line says `'PUT'` `/_users/org.couchdb.user:johndoe`, and it returned a `409` response. The `409` response means that there was an update conflict, which is due to the fact that the name we are passing to the user is the same as the one that already exists. This should be easy enough for us to fix, but we first need to talk about catching errors.

## Catching errors

Luckily, catching errors is relatively easy with the help of our friendly `try...catch` statements. `try...catch` statements allow you to test a block of code for errors. The `try` block contains code that you are attempting to run, and if a problem occurs, the `catch` block is executed.

The syntax of a `try...catch` statement looks similar to the following:

```
try {
  // Code to execute
} catch {
  // A problem occurred, do this
}
```

As I mentioned before, Sag includes an exception class called `SagCouchException`. This class gives us the ability to see how CouchDB responded and then we can take action accordingly.

## Time for action – handling document update conflicts using SagCouchException

We determined in the last section that our code is breaking due to a `409` response. So, let's adjust the signup function in our `classes/user.php` file to handle the exception using `SagCouchException`.

```
public function signup($username, $password) {
  ...

  try {
    $bones->couch->put($this->_id, $this->to_json());
  } catch(SagCouchException $e) {
    if($e->getCode() == "409") {
      $bones->set('error', 'A user with this name already exists.');
      $bones->render('user/signup');
      exit;
    }

  }
}
```

## What just happened?

We used a `try...catch` statement to resolve the duplicate document update conflict that was triggered. By casting it with `(SagCouchException $e)`, we are telling it to only catch `SagCouchExceptions` for now that come through. Once this exception is caught, we are checking to see what code was returned. If it's a code of `409`, we are setting an `error` variable with an error message. Then we need to re-display the user/signup form, so that the user has an opportunity to try the sign up process again. To make sure that no more code is executed after this error, we used the `exit` command so that the application stops right where it is.

We just set an `error` variable. Let's talk about how we can display this variable.

## Showing alerts

In our application, we will display standard notifications in response to user interaction, which we'll call alerts. We just set an error variable to be used in an error alert, but we also would like to be able to show a success message.

# Time for action – showing alerts

In this section, we'll use our existing variables in bones to allow us to show alert messages to our users.

1. Open `lib/bones.php` and create a new function called `display_alert()`. This function will be called to see if the `alert` variable is set. If the `alert` variable is set, we will echo some HTML to show the alert box on the layout.

```php
public function display_alert($variable = 'error') {
  if (isset($this->vars[$variable])) {
  return "<div class='alert alert-" . $variable . "'><a
    class='close' data-dismiss='alert'>x</a>" . $this-
    >vars[$variable] . "</div>";
  }
}
```

2. Add code to `layout.php`, right inside of the container `div` to display the Flash call the `display_flash` function.

```php
<div class="container">
<?php echo $this->display_alert('error'); ?>
<?php echo $this->display_alert('success'); ?>
  <?php include($this->content); ?>
</div>
```

3. Now that we've added these Flash messages, let's go back to our signup POST route in `index.php` and add back in a Flash message that thanks the user for signing up.

```php
$user->signup($app->form('username'), $app->form('password'));

$app->set('success', 'Thanks for Signing Up ' . $user->full_name .
  '!');
$app->render('home');
});
```

## What just happened?

We created a function called `display_alert` that checked to see if a variable with the passed variable was set. If it was set, then we displayed the contents of the variable in an alert box with help from Bootstrap. We then added two lines of code to `layout.php`, so we can display Flash messages for errors and success. Finally, we added a success Flash message to our signup process.

Let's test this all out.

1.  Go back and try to sign up for a user with the username of johndoe again. You'll see this friendly error message, informing you of a problem:

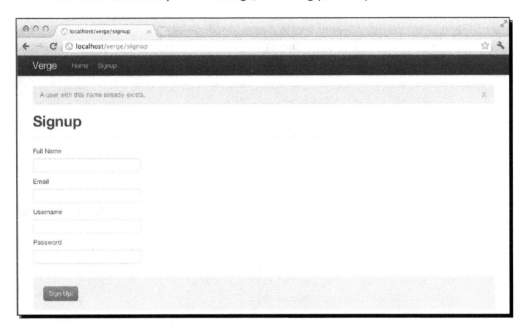

2.  Now, let's test the success alert message. Change the username to johndoe2. Click on **Sign Up!**, and you'll retrieve a nice and green alert.

Even with these simple alerts, our signup form isn't perfect. Random exceptions and errors could occur, and we wouldn't be able to handle them. Even more concerning is that we aren't requiring fields in the form to be filled out. These items need to be on our radar, but we're not going to be able to cover all of that in this book.

Let's move on to talk about user authentication.

# User authentication

Now that we've created users, we definitely need to find a way for them to log in to our system. Luckily, CouchDB and Sag will really do a lot of the heavy lifting for us in this area. In this section we will:

♦ Set up a login form

♦ Learn about sessions, cookies, and how CouchDB and Sag handle authentication for us

♦ Add support for users to log out

♦ Handle the UI differently for logged in and not logged in users

## Setting up for the login form

Let's create some login forms so that our users can log in to our website and use their newly created accounts.

### Have a go hero – setting up the routes and forms for login

We've gone through the process of creating pages, setting up routes, and creating forms a few times before. So, let's see if you can give it a shot by yourself this time. I won't leave you completely without help. I'll first tell you what you need to try to do, and then when you are finished, we'll review and make sure our code matches up.

Here's what you need to do:

1. Create a new page called `user/login.php`.

2. Create new `GET` and `POST` routes for the login page in the `index.php` file.

3. Tell the `GET` route of the login page to render the `user/login` view.

4. Create a form with the `username` and `password` fields using `user/signup.php` as a guide.

5. Add fields called `username` and `password` using the Bootstrap helper and a `submit` button.

While you are doing that, I'm going to watch some TV. Turn over to the next page when you're ready, and we'll see how it went!

Good job! I hope you were able to do that without needing too much help. If you needed to go back and look at the old code for help, don't worry, as that's what a lot of developers end up doing when they are stuck. Let's go through and see how your code matches up to what I have.

The addition to this, your `index.php` file, should look similar to the following:

```php
get('/login', function($app) {
  $app->render('user/login');
});


post('/login', function($app) {

});
```

Your `views/user/login.php` page should look similar to the following:

```php
<div class="page-header">
  <h1>Login</h1>
</div>

<div class="row">
  <div class="span12">
    <form action="<?php echo $this->make_route('/login') ?>"
      method="post">
      <fieldset>
        <?php Bootstrap::make_input('username', 'Username', 'text');
          ?>
        <?php Bootstrap::make_input('password', 'Password',
          'password'); ?>

        <div class="form-actions">
          <button class="btn btn-primary">Login</button>
        </div>
      </fieldset>
    </form>
  </div>
</div>
```

Make sure to update your code to what I have if it's different, so our code matches up down the road.

# Logging in and logging out

Now that we have the forms ready to go, let's talk about what we need to do to make the form actually work. Let's quickly talk about what we are trying to accomplish in the login process.

1.  Sag will connect to the CouchDB `_users` database.

2.  Sag will pass the login information from our PHP directly to CouchDB.

3.  If the login is successful, CouchDB will pass back a cookie that says you are authenticated.

4.  We'll then query CouchDB to grab the currently logged-in username and save it to a session variable for later use.

If you've been developing with other databases for a while, you'll immediately see what's so cool about the login process. CouchDB is handling most of the authentication problems that we usually have to handle ourselves!

Let's go through the login functionality. Luckily, it's much easier than the signup process.

## Time for action – adding functionality for users to log in

We're going to go through this slowly, but I think you're going to love how quickly we're able to add this functionality with all of the code we've written so far.

*1.*  Open `classes/user.php`.

*2.*  Create a `public` function called `login` to which we can pass our plain-text `$password` as a parameter.

```
public function login($password) {
}
```

Create a new bones object and set the database to `_users`.

```
public function login($password) {
  $bones = new Bones();
  $bones->couch->setDatabase('_users');

}
```

**3.** Create a `try...catch` statement for our login code to live in. In the `catch` block, we are going to catch the error code `401`. If it is triggered, we want to tell the user that their login was incorrect.

```
public function login($password) {
  $bones = new Bones();
  $bones->couch->setDatabase('_users');


  try {


  }
  catch(SagCouchException $e) {
    if($e->getCode() == "401") {
      $bones->set('error', ' Incorrect login credentials.');
      $bones->render('user/login');
      exit;
    }
  }
}
```

**4.** Add code to start the session, and then to pass the username and password into CouchDB through Sag. When the user is successfully logged in, grab the current user's username from CouchDB.

```
public function login($password) {
  $bones = new Bones();
  $bones->couch->setDatabase('_users');

  try {
    $bones->couch->login($this->name, $password,
      Sag::$AUTH_COOKIE);
    session_start();
    $_SESSION['username'] = $bones->couch->getSession()->body-
      >userCtx->name;
    session_write_close();
  }
```

## What just happened?

We created a `public` function called `login` in our `user` class that will allow users to log in. We then created a new reference to Bones so that we can access Sag. In order to handle invalid login credentials, we created a `try...catch` block and moved onto handling the `catch` block first. This time, we are checking against an error code of `401`. If the error code matched up, we set the `error` variable to display an error message, rendered the login page, and finally exited the current code.

Next, we worked on the login code by passing the username and the plain-text password to the login method of Sag, along with the setting `Sag::$AUTH_COOKIE`. This parameter is telling us to use CouchDB's cookie authentication. By using cookie authentication, we can handle authentication without having to pass the username and password each time.

Behind the scenes, what's happening is that our username and password are being posted to the `/_session` URL. If the login was a success, it will return a cookie that we can use for each request from here on, in place of the username and password. Luckily, Sag handles all of that for us!

Next, we initialized a session with the `session_start` function, which allows us to set session variables that persist as long as our session exists. We then set a session variable for the username equal to the username of the currently logged in user. We did this by using Sag to grab the session information using `$bones->couch->getSession()`.We then grabbed the body of the response with `->body()` and finally grabbed the current user with `userCtx` and, one step further, to grab the `username` attribute. This all resulted in one line of code as follows:

```
$_SESSION['username'] = $bones->couch->getSession()->body->userCtx->name;
```

Finally, we used `session_write_close` to write the session variable and close down the session. This will increase the speed and decrease the chances of locking. Don't worry; by calling `session_start()` again, we can retrieve our `session` variables again.

Finally, we need to add the login function to our `post` route in `index.php`. Let's do that quickly together.

```
post('/login', function($app) {
    $user = new User();
    $user->name = $app->form('username');
    $user->login($app->form('password'));

    $app->set('success', 'You are now logged in!');
    $app->render('home');
});
```

We could go and test this right now, but let's finish out a few more things so that we can fully test what's going on here.

# Time for action – adding functionality for users to log out

I bet you thought the login script was pretty easy. Wait until you see how easy it is for us to allow users to log out.

**1.** Open `classes/user.php`, and create a `public static` function called `logout`.

```
public static function logout() {
    $bones = new Bones();
    $bones->couch->login(null, null);
    session_start();
    session_destroy();
}
```

**2.** Add a route into the `index.php` file, and have it call the `logout` function.

```
get('/logout', function($app) {
    User::logout();
    $app->redirect('/');
});
```

**3.** Notice that we are calling a new feature inside of Bones – a `redirect` function. In order for this to work, let's add a quick new function at the bottom of our `lib/bones.php` file.

```
public function redirect($path = '/') {
    header('Location: ' . $this->make_route($path));
}
```

## What just happened?

We added a `public static` function called `logout`. The reason we made it `public static` is that it really doesn't matter to us which user is currently logged in. We just need to perform some simple session-level operations. First, we created a `$bones` instantiation as usual, but then, the next part is pretty interesting, so we set `$bones->couch->login(null, null)`. By doing this, we are making the current user an anonymous user, effectively logging them out. Then, we called `session_start` and `session_destroy`. Remember that with `session_start`, we are making our session accessible, then we are destroying it, which removes all the data associated with the current session.

After we were done with the `login` function, we opened up `index.php` and made a call to our `public static` function using `User::logout()`.

Finally, we used a redirect function that we added into the `index.php` file. So, we quickly added a function to Bones, which would allow us to redirect a user to a route by using `make_route`.

# Handling the current user

We'll really want to be able to determine if a user is logged in or not and change the navigation accordingly. Luckily, we can accomplish this in just a few lines of code.

## Time for action – handling the current user

With most of the pieces of the puzzle in place, let's go through the process of changing the layout for users, depending on if they are logged in or not.

1. Let's add a function called `current_user` in `classes/user.php`, so that we can retrieve the current user's username from the session.

```php
public static function current_user() {
  session_start();
  return $_SESSION['username'];
  session_write_close();
}
```

2. Add a public static function called `is_authenticated` into `classes/user.php` so we can see if the user is authenticated or not.

```php
public static function is_authenticated() {
  if (self::current_user()) {
    return true;
  } else {
    return false;
  }
}
```

3. Now that we have our authentication in order, let's tighten up the navigation in `layout.php`, so that different navigation items are displayed depending on if the user is logged in or not.

```php
<ul class="nav">
  <li><a href="<?php echo $this->make_route('/') ?>">Home</a></li>
  <?php if (User::is_authenticated()) { ?>
  <li>
    <a href="<?php echo $this->make_route('/logout') ?>">
      Logout
    </a>
  </li>
  <?php } else { ?>
    <li>
      <a href="<?php echo $this->make_route('/signup') ?>">
        Signup
```

```
        </a>
      </li>
      <li>
        <a href="<?php echo $this->make_route('/login') ?>">
          Login
        </a>
      </li>
    <?php } ?>
  </ul>
```

## What just happened?

We started by creating a `public static` function called `current_user` that will retrieve the username that is stored inside the session. We then created another `public static` function called `is_authenticated`. This function checks `current_user` for a username, and, if it's available, the user is logged in. If it's not, the user is not currently logged in.

Finally, we quickly went into our layout so that we could show links to home and log out if a user is logged in, and links to home, signup, login if the user is not currently logged in.

Let's test this out:

1. Open your browser to the login page by going to `http://localhost/verge/login`. Notice that the header is displaying **Home**, **Signup**, and **Login** for you because you aren't currently logged in.

2. Log in with the credentials of one of your user accounts. You'll receive a nice alert message, and the header changes to display **Home** and **Logout**.

3. Finally, click on **Logout**, and you'll see everything turn back to the original state with **Home**, **Signup**, and **Login** in the navigation.

# Summary

I hope you're blown away by how much we've been able to accomplish in this chapter. Our application is really starting to come together.

Specifically, we covered:

- How to dramatically improve the interface by using Bootstrap from Twitter
- How to create additional fields on top of existing CouchDB user documents
- How to handle errors and debug issues with logs
- How to completely build out the ability, so that users can sign up, log in, and log out of our application with the help of Sag and CouchDB

This is just the beginning of our application. We still have a lot to do. In the next chapter, we will start to work on a user profile and work on the creation of new documents in CouchDB. These documents will be our users' posts.

# 7

# User Profiles and Modeling Posts

*With the base of our application created, we have allowed users to sign up and log in to our application. This is a huge part of any application, but we are still missing the creation of content that we can connect to the user accounts. We'll go through all of it in this chapter!*

In this chapter we will:

- Create a user profile to publicly display a user's information
- Clean up the profile using Bootstrap
- Handle all kinds of exceptions
- Discuss modeling of posts and relationships in CouchDB
- Create a form to create posts from the logged-in user's profile

With our road mapped out for us, let's move on to talk about the user profile!

## User profile

The main attraction of any social network is a user's profile; the user profile usually displays the basic information of a user and shows any content that they have created.

By the end of this section, our user profiles will work as follows:

- If a visitor goes to `http://localhost/verge/user/johndoe`, our routing system will match it with the route `/user/:username`
- The `index.php` file will take `johndoe` as the value for `username`, and pass it to the `User` class in an attempt to find the user document with a matching ID

◆ If johndoe is found, index.php will display a profile with the information for johndoe

◆ If johndoe is not found, the visitor will see a 404 error, meaning that the user with that username does not exist

## Finding a user with routes

In order to find users, we'll first need to create a function that will take the username as a parameter and return a user object if it is a valid one.

## Time for action – getting single user documents

As you might remember, in *Chapter 3, Getting Started with CouchDB and Futon*, we were able to retrieve a document from CouchDB just by passing the ID of the document we wanted. We are going to do the same thing this time to find a user's information using Sag. One important thing to note is that we'll have to make sure that when we look for users using their ID, we need to prepend it with the org.couchdb.user: namespace.

Let's start by opening classes/user.php and scrolling to the bottom.

1. Add a public static function called get_by_username().

```
public static function get_by_username() {

}
```

2. In order to find a user by ID, we need to allow our function to accept the parameter $username.

```
public static function get_by_username($username = null) {

}
```

3. Now, let's set the database to instantiate Bones and a proxy Sag. Remember, we're dealing with the _users database, so we'll need to log in with the admin privileges.

```
public static function get_by_username($username = null) {
    $bones = new Bones();
    $bones->couch->setDatabase('_users');
    $bones->couch->login(ADMIN_USER, ADMIN_PASSWORD);
}
```

**4.** Now that we can connect to the _users database, let's issue a get call through Sag that will return a user by adding org.couchdb.user: to the passed username.

```
public static function get_by_username($username = null) {
  $bones = new Bones()
  $bones->couch->login(ADMIN_USER, ADMIN_PASSWORD);
  $bones->couch->setDatabase('_users');
  $user = new User();

  $document = $bones->couch->get('org.couchdb.user:' . $username)-
    >body;
  $user->_id = $document->_id;
  $user->name = $document->name;
  $user->email = $document->email;
  $user->full_name = $document->full_name;

  return $user;
}
```

## What just happened?

We created a public static function called get_by_username that allows us to pass in $username. To actually get the document, we need to use our ADMIN_USER and ADMIN_PASSWORD constants to access the _users database. In order for us to return a user object, we needed to create a new user object called $user. We then used Sag's get call to identify the document by ID and return it as a stdClass object called $document. We then grabbed the values from the document variable and passed them into the corresponding values on the $user object. Finally, we returned the user document to wherever the function was called from.

Now that we have a function to handle the finding of a user by the username, let's create a route in index.php that will pass a username to this function.

## Time for action – creating a route for user profiles

We are going to create a route so that people can see a profile by going to a unique URL. This will be the first time that we'll really utilize our routing system's ability to handle route variables.

**1.** Open index.php, and create a get route for a user profile by entering the following code:

```
get('/user/:username', function($app) {

});
```

**2.** Let's use the route variable `:username` to tell us the username that we want to find; we'll pass this to the `get_by_username` function we created in the `User` class. Finally, we'll pass the returned `user` object to the view in the `user` variable:

```
get('/user/:username', function($app) {
  $app->set('user', User::get_by_username($app-
    >request('username')));
});
```

**3.** Lastly, we'll render the `user/profile.php` view, which we will create shortly.

```
get('/user/:username', function($app) {
    $app->set('user', User::get_by_username($app-
    >request('username')));
    $app->render('user/profile');
});
```

## What just happened?

We did a lot in just four lines of code! First, we defined the user profile route by using `route /user/:username`. Next, we created a piece of code that passes `:username` from the `route` variable to the `get_by_username` function in our `user` class. The `get_by_username` function will return an object containing the information of a user, and we sent that to our view using `$app->set('user')`. Finally, we rendered the user profile.

Let's go on to create the user profile so that we can see our hard work in action!

## Time for action – creating the user profile

We're going to clean up the `user` view a few times in this chapter. But, let's start by just dumping out all of the user document content into our view.

**1.** Create a view called `user/profile.php` inside the `views` directory in our `working` folder.

**2.** Make a simple header for the profile with the following HTML:

```
<div class="page-header">
  <h1>User Profile</h1>
</div>
```

**3.** Since we don't have much of a design yet, let's just use `var_dump` to show all of the contents of the `User` document:

```
<div class="page-header">
  <h1>User Profile</h1>
```

```
    </div>

    <div class="container">
      <div class="row">
        <?php var_dump($user); ?>
      </div>
    </div>
```

# What just happened?

We just created a very basic user profile with a header to tell us that this page is the user profile. Then, we used `var_dump` to display all of the contents of the `user` object. `var_dump` is a general PHP function that outputs structured information about a variable or object and is very useful when you just want to make sure that things are working properly.

## Testing it out

Now that we have a simple user profile setup, let's see how it turned out.

1. Open your browser, and go to `http://localhost/verge/user/johndoe`.

2. Your browser will show you the following:

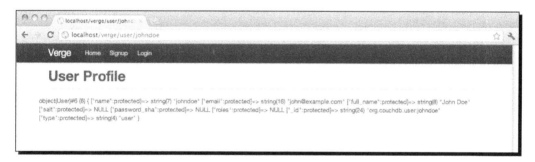

Not too shabby, but of course we'll need to clean up the format of this data shortly. But, for now, let's make sure to commit our changes to Git.

## Adding your changes to Git

In this section, we started to create a user profile and output a user's information directly from CouchDB. Let's add all of our changes to Git, so that we can track our progress.

1. Open Terminal.

2. Type the following command to change directories to our working directory.

   ```
   cd /Library/Webserver/Documents/verge/
   ```

3. We only added one file, `views/user/profile.php`, so let's tell Git to add this file to source control.

   ```
   git add views/user/profile.php
   ```

4. Give `Git` a description of what we've done since our last commit.

   ```
   git commit -am 'Created the get_by_username function, a basic user
   profile, and a route to display it'
   ```

# Fixing some problems

You may have already noticed that we ignored a potential issue with our user profiles, we aren't gracefully handling what happens when a user profile isn't found.

For example:

If you were to go to `http://localhost/verge/user/someone`, your browser would display this very unfriendly error message:

# Finding errors

In *Chapter 6*, we used the `tail` command through Terminal to look at Apache's error logs. We're going to do the same thing again. Let's take a look at the log from Apache and see if we can figure out what went wrong.

## Time for action – examining Apache's log

In *Chapter 6*, we tried to locate our Apache log first. By default, it is saved at `/private/var/log/apache2/error_log`. If in the previous chapter you found it was located somewhere else, you can find its location again by typing `grep ErrorLog /etc/apache2/httpd.conf`.

Let's find out what the problem was.

**1.** Open Terminal.

**2.** Retrieve the last few lines of the log by running the following command:

```
tail /private/var/log/apache2/error_log
```

**3.** The log will show you a bunch of things, but the most important message is this one, that says PHP Fatal error. Yours might be slightly different, but the overall message is the same.

```
[Wed Sep 28 09:29:49 2011] [error] [client 127.0.0.1] PHP Fatal
error:  Uncaught exception 'SagCouchException' with message
'CouchDB Error: not_found (missing)' in /Library/WebServer/
Documents/verge/lib/sag/src/Sag.php:1221\nStack trace:\n#0 /
Library/WebServer/Documents/verge/lib/sag/src/Sag.php(206): Sag-
>procPacket('GET', '/_users/org.cou...')\n#1 /Library/WebServer/
Documents/verge/classes/user.php(81): Sag->get('org.couchdb.
use...')\n#2 /Library/WebServer/Documents/verge/index.php(44):
User::get_by_username('someone')\n#3 /Library/WebServer/Documents/
verge/lib/bones.php(91): {closure}(Object(Bones))\n#4 /Library/
WebServer/Documents/verge/lib/bones.php(13): Bones::register('/
user/:username', Object(Closure), 'GET')\n#5 /Library/
WebServer/Documents/verge/index.php(46): get('/user/:username',
Object(Closure))\n#6 {main}\n  thrown in /Library/WebServer/
Documents/verge/lib/sag/src/Sag.php on line 1221
```

## What just happened?

We used a tail command to return the last few lines of the Apache log. If you look closely at the log, you'll see the CouchDB error. To be more specific, the error is as follows:

```
error:  Uncaught exception 'SagCouchException' with message 'CouchDB
Error: not_found (missing)'
```

This message means that CouchDB isn't happy with what we are doing, and Sag is throwing an error in the form of a SagCouchException. In order for us to appropriately handle SagCouchException, we need to add some code to our call to Sag.

In the previous chapter, we fixed an error by checking for the status code and matching it with a resolution. We can keep doing this, but eventually errors are going to occur that we're not aware of. From here on out, when an unhandled exception occurs, we want to display a friendly error message so that we can debug it.

In the next section, we will use Bones to help us show an exception page.

# Handling 500 errors

What we're really looking to solve here is how we want to handle 500 errors in our application. **500 errors** refer to the HTTP status code 500, which is an "Internal Server Error". Generally, this means that something happened, and we didn't handle it properly.

## Time for action – handling 500 errors with Bones

Let's start by creating a simple view that will display errors to us.

1.  Let's start by creating a new folder called error inside our views directory.

2.  Create a new view called 500.php, and place it into the errors folder (views/error/500.php).

3.  Add the following code to the 500.php output information on the exception:

```
<div class="hero-unit">
  <h1>An Error Has Occurred</h1>
  <p>
    <strong>Code:</strong><?php echo $exception->getCode(); ?>
  </p>
  <p>
    <strong>Message:</strong>
    <?php echo $exception->getMessage(); ?>
  </p>
  <p><strong>Exception:</strong> <?php echo $exception; ?></p>
</div>
```

4.  Add a function called error500 in lib/bones.php that will allow us to display 500 errors easily around our application.

```
public function error500($exception) {
      $this->set('exception', $exception);
      $this->render('error/500');
      exit;
}
```

## *What just happened?*

We created a new folder in our `views` directory called `error`, which will house all of the error views that we'll use in our application. We then created a new view called `500.php` to display our exceptions in a nice and friendly way. Exceptions are a built-in class that Sag extends upon, using the `SagCouchException` class. With this, it's easy for us to talk directly to this exception class in our view. This `Exception` class has a lot of properties. But, in this application, we are just going to display the code, message, and the exception, represented in a string format. Lastly, we created a function in Bones to allow us to pass the exception in, so that we can display it in the view. In this function, we passed the exception to the `error/500` view, and then used `exit`, which tells PHP to stop doing anything else in our application. This stops our application from doing anything else because a problem occurred.

## Time for action – handling exceptions

Now that we can handle exceptions, let's add some code to the `get_by_username` function, so that we can take a deeper look at our problem.

1. Let's open `classes/user.php`, and add a `try...catch` statement around our Sag call to make sure that we can handle any errors that occur.

```
public static function get_by_username($username = null) {
  $bones = new Bones();
  $bones->couch->login(ADMIN_USER, ADMIN_PASSWORD);
  $bones->couch->setDatabase('_users');

  $user = new User();

  try {
    $document = $bones->couch->get('org.couchdb.user:' .
      $username)->body;
    $user->_id = $document->_id;
    $user->name = $document->name;
    $user->email = $document->email;
    $user->full_name = $document->full_name;

    return $user;
  } catch (SagCouchException $e) {

  }
}
```

**2.** Now that we are catching errors, let's add in our `error500` function.

```
public static function get_by_username($username = null) {
  $bones = new Bones();
  $bones->couch->login(ADMIN_USER, ADMIN_PASSWORD);
  $bones->couch->setDatabase('_users');

  $user = new User();

  try {
    $document = $bones->couch->get('org.couchdb.user:' .
      $username)->body;
    $user->_id = $document->_id;
    $user->name = $document->name;
    $user->email = $document->email;
    $user->full_name = $document->full_name;

    return $user;
  } catch (SagCouchException $e) {
    $bones->error500($e);
  }
}
```

**3.** While we are in `classes/user.php`, let's catch a few more possible exceptions. Let's start with the `public` function signup.

```
public function signup($username, $password) {
  $bones = new Bones();
  $bones->couch->setDatabase('_users');
  $bones->couch->login(ADMIN_USER, ADMIN_PASSWORD);

  $this->roles = array();
  $this->name = preg_replace('/[^a-z0-9-]/', '',
    strtolower($username));
  $this->_id = 'org.couchdb.user:' . $this->name;
  $this->salt = $bones->couch->generateIDs(1)->body->uuids[0];
  $this->password_sha = sha1($password . $this->salt);

  try {
    $bones->couch->put($this->_id, $this->to_json());
  }
  catch(SagCouchException $e) {
    if($e->getCode() == "409") {
      $bones->set('error', 'A user with this name already
        exists.');
      $bones->render('user/signup');
```

```
    } else {
      $bones->error500($e);
    }
  }
}
```

**4.** Next, let's add to the `catch` statement in our public function login.

```
public function login($password) {
  $bones = new Bones();
  $bones->couch->setDatabase('_users');

  try {
    $bones->couch->logiBn($this->name, $password,
      Sag::$AUTH_COOKIE);
    session_start();
    $_SESSION['username'] = $bones->couch->getSession()->body-
      >userCtx->name;
    session_write_close();
  }
  catch(SagCouchException $e) {
    if($e->getCode() == "401") {
      $bones->set('error', 'Incorrect login credentials.');
      $bones->render('user/login');
      exit;
    } else {
      $bones->error500($e);
    }
  }
}
```

## What just happened?

Now that we can gracefully handle exceptions, we went through our `User` class and added the ability to throw a `500` error when something unexpected occurred. On calls where we are already expecting certain problems, we can use an `if...else` statement to trigger a `500` error if something unexpected happens.

## Testing our exception handler

Let's try again to see if we can get to the bottom of the exception.

1. Go to `http://localhost/verge/user/someone`.

2. You will now see a much friendlier error page, which tells us the code, message, and the full error that you would see in the error logs.

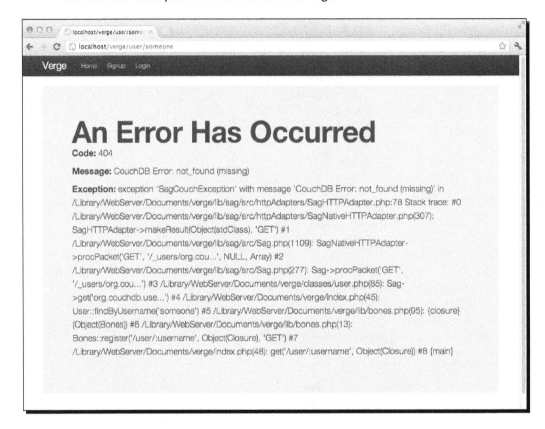

It is much easier for us to figure out what's going on from this. While we are in the process of debugging our application, this page will be of great use to us to track down what errors are occurring.

By looking at this piece of code, we can tell that CouchDB is throwing us a 404 error. We might expect that this error would occur because we're looking for a user document that doesn't exist. Let's dig further into what a 404 error is and how we can handle it.

# Showing 404 errors

A 404 error refers to the HTTP status code 404, meaning "Not Found". A 404 error usually occurs when you try to access something that doesn't exist, such as going to an incorrect URL. In our case, we are receiving a 404 error because we are trying to find a CouchDB document that doesn't exist.

## 404 if user isn't found

`404` errors are a special kind of errors that we'll see in different places around our application. Let's create another error page that we can use whenever `404` errors occur.

## Time for action: handling 404 errors with Bones

Let's create a view for `404` errors that we can use around our application.

*1.* Start by creating a new view in our `views/error/` directory called `404.php`.

*2.* Let's add some very basic code to `404.php` that will inform the visitor that our application couldn't find the requested page.

```
<div class="hero-unit">
  <h1>Page Not Found</h1>
</div>
```

*3.* In order for us to render this view, let's add another function called `error404` into our `lib/bones.php` file. This function will nicely display `404` errors for us.

```
public function error404() {
  $this->render('error/404');
  exit;
}
```

## What just happened?

We created a simple view, called `404.php`, that we can show any time a `404` error occurs in our application. We then created a simple function called `error404` in `lib/bones.php` that renders `error/404.php` and terminates the current script so no further actions occur.

## Showing 404 errors for unknown users

Now that we have our `404` error handler, let's display it when the `404` error occurs in the `get_by_username` function inside of `classes/user.php`.

Open `classes/user.php`, and alter the `get_by_username` function to match the following:

```
public static function get_by_username($username = null) {
  $bones = new Bones();
  $bones->couch->login(ADMIN_USER, ADMIN_PASSWORD);
  $bones->couch->setDatabase('_users');

  $user = new User();
```

```
    try {
$document = $bones->couch->get('org.couchdb.user:' . $username)-
  >body;
$user->_id = $document->_id;
$user->name = $document->name;
$user->email = $document->email;
$user->full_name = $document->full_name;

return $user;
  } catch (SagCouchException $e) {
    if($e->getCode() == "404") {
      $bones->error404();
    } else {
      $bones->error500($e);
    }
  }
}
```

## Hooking up 404 all around the site

The interesting thing about 404 errors is that they can happen any time a visitor passes a route that Bones doesn't understand. So, let's add code right into Bones that will handle this for us.

## Time for action – handling 404 errors with Bones

Let's add some simple code around lib/bones.php and index.php that will allow us to handle 404 errors.

1.  Open lib/bones.php, and a create a function inside the Bones class called resolve that we can call at the end of our routes and determine if a route was ever found.

    ```
    public static function resolve() {
      if (!static::$route_found) {
        $bones = static::get_instance();
        $bones->error404();
      }
    }
    ```

2.  Go to the top of lib/bones.php, and create a function called resolve outside the Bones class (such as get, post, put, or delete) that we can call outside anywhere.

    ```
    function resolve() {
      Bones::resolve();
    }
    ```

**3.** All that's left for us to do is add a line of code at the very bottom of `index.php` that can be called if no routes are found. As you add more routes, make sure that `resolve()` is always at the end of the file.

```
get('/user/:username', function($app) {
  $app->set('user', User::get_by_username($app-
    >request('username')));
  $app->render('user/profile');
});

resolve();
```

## *What just happened?*

We created a function called `resolve` that is executed at the bottom of our `index.php` file after all of our routes. This function serves as a "clean up" function that will be executed if no routes match up. If no routes match, resolve will display a `404` error to the visitor and terminate the current script.

## Testing it out

Now that we're gracefully handling `404` errors, let's test it out and see what happens.

1. Open your browser, and go to `http://localhost/verge/user/anybody`.

2. Your browser will show you the following:

Great! Our `User` class is forwarding us a `404` error because of the code we added in the `get_by_username` function.

3. Next, let's check that our `index.php` will forward us a `404` error if it can't find the requested route.

4. Open your browser to `http://localhost/verge/somecrazyurl`.

5. Your browser will display the following:

Perfect! Our 404 error handler is working exactly like we need it to. If we ever need to use it again, all we need to do is call error404 in our Bones class, and we're all set!

## Giving users a link to their profile

In most social networks, once you are logged in, you are shown a link to see the currently logged in users' profiles. Let's open view/layout.php and add a My Profile link to our navigation.

```php
<ul class="nav">
  <li><a href="<?php echo $this->make_route('/') ?>">Home</a></li>
  <?php if (User::is_authenticated()) { ?>
    <li>
      <a href="<?php echo $this->make_route('/user/' .
        User::current_user()) ?>">
        My Profile
      </a>
    </li>
    <li>
      <a href="<?php echo $this->make_route('/logout') ?>">
        Logout
      </a>
    </li>
  <?php } else { ?>
    <li>
      <a href="<?php echo $this->make_route('/signup') ?>">
        Signup
      </a>
    </li>
    <li>
```

```
    <a href="<?php echo $this->make_route('/login') ?>">
      Login
    </a>
  </li>
<?php } ?>
</ul>
```

# Creating a better profile with Bootstrap

It's starting to bug me that our profile isn't all that nicely put together, and we're going to need to add to this more later in the chapter. Let's prepare our user profile so that we can nicely show a user's information and posts.

## Time for action – checking whether a user is currently logged in

We'll need to be able to figure out if the profile a user is looking at is their own. So, let's add a variable to our view that tells us if that is the case.

***1.*** Open `index.php`, and add a variable called `is_current_user` that will determine if the profile that you are viewing is equal to the currently logged-in user.

```php
get('/user/:username', function($app) {
  $app->set('user', User::get_by_username($app-
    >request('username')));
  $app->set('is_current_user', ($app->request('username') ==
User::current_user() ? true : false));
  $app->render('user/profile');
});
```

***2.*** Let's change the code in the header of `views/user/profile.php` so that we can output the user's full name as well as `This is you!`, if it's the current user's profile.

```php
<div class="page-header">
  <h1><?php echo $user->full_name; ?>
    <?php if ($is_current_user) { ?>
      <code>This is you!</code>
    <?php } ?>
  </h1>
</div>
```

## What just happened?

We used a shorthand operation called `ternary`. A `ternary` operation is short hand for an `if-else` statement. In this case, we are saying that if the username passed from the route is equal to that of the currently logged-in user, then return `true`, otherwise return `false`. Then, we go into our profile and display `This is you!` if the `is_current_user` variable is set to `true`.

## Cleaning up the profile's design

Again, Bootstrap will come to the rescue by allowing us to clean up our profile with limited code.

1. Let's start by splitting our row `div` into two columns with the following code:

```
<div class="page-header">
  <h1><?php echo $user->full_name; ?>
    <?php if ($is_current_user) { ?>
      <code>This is you!</code>
    <?php } ?>
  </h1>
</div>

<div class="container">
  <div class="row">
    <div class="span4">
      <div class="well sidebar-nav">
        <ul class="nav nav-list">
          <li><h3>User Information</h3>
        </ul>
      </div>
    </div>
    <div class="span8">
        <h2>Posts</h2>
    </div>
  </div>
</div>
```

2. Let's output the user's information into the left column by adding more list items into the unordered list.

```
<div class="container">
  <div class="row">
    <div class="span4">
      <div class="well sidebar-nav">
        <ul class="nav nav-list">
          <li><h3>User Information</h3></li>
          <li><b>Username:</b> <?php echo $user->name; ?></li>
          <li><b>Email:</b> <?php echo $user->email; ?></li>
        </ul>
```

```
            </div>
        </div>
        <div class="span8">
            <h2>Posts</h2>
        </div>
    </div>
</div>
```

## Let's check out our new profile

With that, our new and improved profile has come to life! Let's check it out.

1.  Open your browser to the URL of the `johndoe` user by going to `http://localhost/verge/user/johndoe`.

2.  Your browser will show you a nicely remodeled user profile.

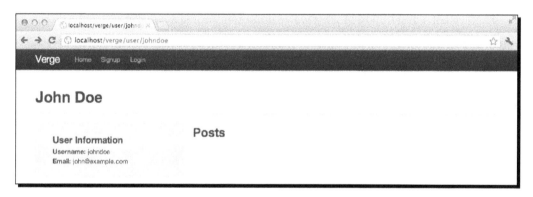

3.  Now, let's check to make sure our `$is_current_user` variable is working correctly too. To do that, log in with `johndoe` as the username, and go to `http://localhost/verge/user/johndoe`.

4.  Your browser will show you the user profile, along with a nice message telling you that this is your profile.

Awesome! Our profile is really starting to come together. This is a big landmark in our application. So, let's make sure we commit our changes to Git.

## Adding your changes to Git

In this section, we added support to cleanly handle exceptions and also spruced up the user profile. Let's add all of our changes to Git so that we can track our progress.

1. Open Terminal.
2. Type the following command to change directories to our `working` directory:

   ```
   cd /Library/Webserver/Documents/verge/
   ```

3. We added a few files in this section. So, let's add them all into source control.

   ```
   git add .
   ```

4. Give Git a description of what we've done since our last commit.

   ```
   git commit -am 'Added 404 and 500 error exception handling and
   spruced up the layout of the user profile'
   ```

# Posts

We have a placeholder for posts on our profile. But, let's get into filling it in with some real content. We are going to do this by allowing users to post small pieces of content and by having them tied to the user account.

## Modeling Posts

Let's talk through what needs to happen in order for us to save posts to CouchDB and relate them to a user. Before we get into how to do this with CouchDB, let's try to bring it into perspective by looking at how we would do it with MySQL.

### How to model posts in MySQL

If we were modeling this relationship for MySQL (or another RDBMS), it might look similar to the following screenshot:

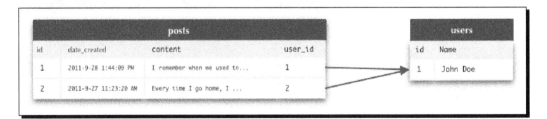

In a nutshell, this diagram shows a `posts` table that has a foreign key `user_id` that references the `id` of the users table. This one-to-many relationship is a common occurrence in most applications and, in this case, means that one user can have many posts.

Now that we've looked at a familiar diagram, let's look at the same relationship as it pertains to CouchDB.

## How to model posts in CouchDB

Surprisingly enough, CouchDB handles relationships in a very similar fashion. You might be thinking to yourself, Wait a minute, I thought you said it wasn't a relational database. Keep in mind that no matter what database you are using, chances are there will be commonalities with how they handle relationships. Let's look at how CouchDB would illustrate the same data and model.

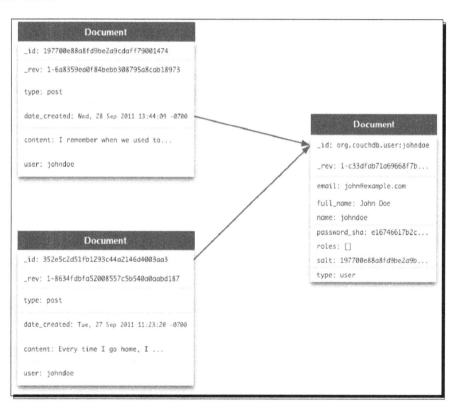

This is pretty similar, right? The biggest difference, as always, is that in the relational database, the data is stored in set rows and columns, while in CouchDB, they are stored in self-contained documents with a schema-less set of keys and values. Regardless of which way you look at the data, the relationship remains the same, that is, a post is connected to a user by way of a reference to that user's ID.

Just to make sure we're on the same page, let's walk through each of the fields in the `post` documents and make sure we understand what they are.

- `_id` is the unique identifier of the document.
- `_rev` is the revision identifier of the document. We touched on revisions in Chapter 3, if you'd like to revisit this concept.
- `type` tells us what kind of document we are looking at. In this case, every `post` document will be equal to `post`.
- `date_created` is the timestamp of when the document was created.
- `content` contains any text that we want to have inside our posts.
- `user` contains the username of the user that created the post and refers back to the `_users` document. Interestingly enough, we do not need to put `org.couchdb.user` in this field, because CouchDB is actually going to look at the username.

Now that we've defined the values that we need to save to CouchDB, we are ready to model it in a new class: `Post`.

## Have a go hero – setting up the Post class

Creating the `Post` class will be very similar to our `User` class. If you feel confident enough, try creating the basic class by yourself.

Here's what you need to do:

1. Create a new class called `post.php` that extends the `Base` class.
2. Create variables for each of the required fields defined earlier.
3. Add a `construct` function to define the type of the document.

When you are done, continue reading on the next page, and make sure your work matches up with mine.

Let's check to see how everything turned out.

You should have created a new file called `post.php` and placed it in the `classes` directory in our `working` folder. The contents of `post.php` should look similar to the following:

```php
<?php

class Post extends Base
{
  protected $date_created;
  protected $content;
```

```
   protected $user;

   public function __construct() {
     parent::__construct('post');
   }
 }
```

That's all we need to handle post documents in PHP. Now that we have the class built, let's move on to creating posts.

# Creating posts

Creating posts is going to be a piece of cake for us now. All we need to do is add a few lines of code, and it'll be sitting in the database.

## Time for action – making a function to handle Post creation

Let's create a public function called `create` that will handle the creation of posts for our application.

1.  Open `classes/post.php`, and scroll to the bottom. Here, we'll create a new public function called `create`.

    ```
    public function create() {

    }
    ```

2.  Let's start by getting a new instance of Bones, and then setting the variables of the current `post` object.

    ```
    public function create() {
      $bones = new Bones();

      $this->_id = $bones->couch->generateIDs(1)->body->uuids[0];
      $this->date_created = date('r');
      $this->user = User::current_user();
    }
    ```

3.  Finally, let's put the document to CouchDB, using Sag.

    ```
    public function create() {
      $bones = new Bones();

      $this->_id = $bones->couch->generateIDs(1)->body->uuids[0];
      $this->date_created = date('r');
    ```

```
        $this->user = User::current_user();

        $bones->couch->put($this->_id, $this->to_json());
    }
```

4.  Let's wrap the call to CouchDB with a `try...catch` statement, and inside of the `catch` statement, let's bounce it to a `500` error as we've done before.

```
public function create() {
    $bones = new Bones();

    $this->_id = $bones->couch->generateIDs(1)->body->uuids[0];
    $this->date_created = date('r');
    $this->user = User::current_user();

    try {
        $bones->couch->put($this->_id, $this->to_json());
    }
    catch(SagCouchException $e) {
        $bones->error500($e);
    }
}
```

## What just happened?

We just made a function called `create` that enables us to create a new `Post` document. We started by instantiating an object of Bones, so that we can use Sag. Next, we used Sag to grab a `UUID` for us to use as the ID of our `post`. Then, we used `date('r')` to output the date into a `RFC 2822` format (which is what CouchDB and JavaScript like) and saved it to the post's `date_created` variable. Then, we set the user of the post to the current user's username.

With all of the fields set, we used Sag's `put` command to save the post document to CouchDB. Finally, to make sure we didn't run into any errors, we wrapped the `put` command in a `try...catch` statement. In the `catch` segment, we passed the user on to Bones' `error500` function if something went wrong. That's it! We can now create posts in our application. All we have left is to make a form in our user profile.

## Time for action – making a form to enable Post creation

Let's code the form for post creation right into our user's profile page. This form will only show up if the logged-in user is looking at their own profile.

1.  Open `user/profile.php`.

**2.** Let's first check to see if the profile the user is looking at is their own.

```
<div class="span8">
  <?php if ($is_current_user) { ?>
    <h2>Create a new post</h2>
  <?php } ?>

  <h2>Posts</h2>
</div>
```

**3.** Next, let's add a form that will allow the currently logged-in user to make posts.

```
<div class="span8">
  <?php if ($is_current_user) { ?>
    <h2>Create a new post</h2>
    <form action="<?php echo $this->make_route('/post')?>"
      method="post">
      <textarea id="content" name="content" class="span8"
        rows="3">
      </textarea>
      <button id="create_post" class="btn btn-primary">Submit
      </button>
    </form>
  <?php } ?>

  <h2>Posts</h2>
</div>
```

## What just happened?

We used the $is_current_user variable to determine if the user viewing the profile is equal to the currently logged-in user. Next, we created a form that posts to the post route (which we'll create next). In the form, we've put a textarea with id of content and a submit button to actually post the form.

Now that we have everything all ready to go, let's finish off the post creation by creating a route called post in our index.php file to handle the post route.

## Time for action – creating a route and handling the creation of the Post

In order to actually create a post, we'll need to create a route and handle the form input.

1. Open `index.php`.

2. Create a basic `post` route, and call it `post`.

   ```
   post('/post', function($app) {

   });
   ```

3. Inside our `post` route, let's accept the value of the passed value `content` and use the `create` function on our `Post` class to actually create the post. Once the post is created, we'll redirect the user back to their profile.

   ```
   post('/post', function($app) {
     $post = new Post();
     $post->content = $app->form('content');
     $post->create();
     $app->redirect('/user/' . User::current_user());
   });
   ```

4. We've done quite a bit to make sure that the user is authenticated when creating a post, but let's triple check that the user is authenticated here. If it turns out that they aren't authenticated, our application will forward them to the user login page with an error message.

   ```
   post('/post', function($app) {
     if (User::is_authenticated()) {
       $post = new Post();
       $post->content = $app->form('content');
       $post->create();
       $app->redirect('/user/' . User::current_user());
     } else {
       $app->set('error', 'You must be logged in to do that.');
       $app->render('user/login');
     }
   });
   ```

## *What just happened?*

In this section, we made a post route for the route post (sorry, that's a confusing sentence to decipher). Inside the post route, we instantiated a Post object, and set it's instance's variable content equal to the content textarea from the posted form. Next, we created the post by calling the public create function. After the post was saved, we redirected the user back to his/her own profile. Lastly, we added functionality around the whole route that checked to make sure the user was logged in. If they aren't, we'll bounce them to the login page and ask them to log in to perform this action.

# Test it out

Now that we've programmed everything we need to create a post, let's go through it step by step to test it.

1. Start by logging in as johndoe and going to his profile by opening your browser to http://localhost/verge/user/johndoe.

2. Your browser will show you a user profile just as we've seen before, but this time you'll see the post form.

3. Type some content into the text area. I typed I don't like peanut butter, but you can make it say whatever you want.

4. When you are done, click on the **Submit** button.

5. You've been forwarded back to the user profile of johndoe, but you can't see any posts yet. So, let's log into Futon to make sure the post was created.

6. Go to the verge database in Futon by going to http://localhost:5984/_utils/database.html?verge.

7. Sweet! There's a document here; let's open it up and look at the contents.

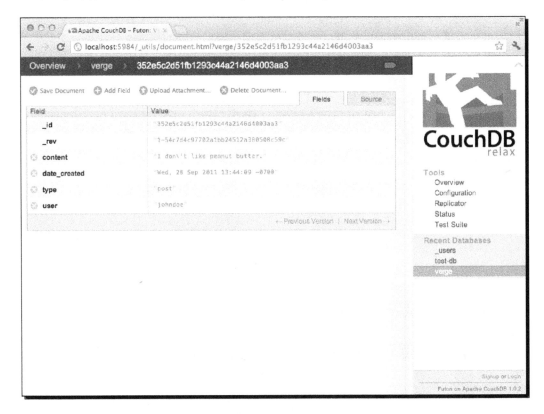

This worked out perfectly! When a user is logged in, they can create a post by going to their profile and submitting the **Create a new post** form.

## Adding your changes to Git

In this section, we added a function to create posts based upon our `Post` model. We then added a form to the user profile so that users can actually create posts. Let's add all of our changes to Git so that we can track our progress.

1. Open Terminal.

2. Type the following command to change directories to our `working` directory:

   ```
   cd /Library/Webserver/Documents/verge/
   ```

3. We added the `classes/post.php` file, so let's add that file into source control:

   ```
   git add classes/post.php
   ```

4. Give `Git` a description of what we've done since our last commit:

   ```
   git commit -am 'Added a Post class, built out basic post creation
   into the user profile. Done with chapter 7.'
   ```

5. I know I said that I wouldn't remind you again, but I'm only human. Let's push these changes up to GitHub.

   ```
   git push origin master
   ```

# Wrapping up

Believe it or not, this is all the code we're going to write in this chapter. Put away your protest signs that say, "We haven't even queried the users' posts yet!" The reason we are stopping here is that CouchDB has a really interesting way of listing and handling documents. In order to get into that discussion, we'll need to define how to use **Design Documents** for views and validation. Luckily, that's exactly what we'll cover in the next chapter!

In the meantime, let's quickly recap what we accomplished in this chapter.

# Summary

In this chapter, we covered the creation of a user profile to display a user's information, how to handle exceptions gracefully and display to users the `500` and `404` error pages, how to model Posts in CouchDB, and finally, the creation of a form to create posts for the logged-in user.

As I said, in the next chapter, we're going to touch on some pretty cool concepts that CouchDB brings to the table. It's probably the most complicated chapter in this book, but it'll be a lot of fun.

# 8
# Using Design Documents for Views and Validation

*So far, our application is not dramatically different from what you might do if you were using MySQL or some other relational database. But, in this chapter, we're really going to turn up the heat on what we can do with CouchDB by using it to handle a lot of things that may have been pain points with relational databases in the past.*

In this chapter we will:

◆ Define design documents

◆ Learn about views and how to use them to query data

◆ Discover the power of MapReduce functions

◆ Play with CouchDB's `validation` function

Let's not waste time, and move right into talking about design documents.

## Design documents

**Design documents** are one of the special things that CouchDB has in its arsenal that you might not expect from a database. On the surface, design documents look the same as regular documents. They have the standard fields: `_id` and `_rev`, and can be created, read, updated, and deleted. But unlike normal documents, they contain application code in the form of JavaScript and have a specific structure. This JavaScript can drive validation, display views with `map` and `reduce` functions, and a whole lot more. We'll touch on each of these features and how to use them shortly.

# A basic design document

A basic design document might look similar to the following:

```
{
  "_id" : "_design/application",
  "_rev" : "3-71c0b0bd73a9c9a45ea738f1e9612798",

  "views" : {
    "example" : {
      "map" : "function(doc){ emit(doc._id, doc)}"
    }
  }
}
```

The `_id` and `_rev` should look familiar, but unlike other documents so far, the `_id` has a readable name: `_design/example`. Design documents are identified as such by having `_design` in the name. So, it's important that you follow this format.

Moving on from `_id` and `_rev`, you'll notice the key views. Views are a big part of design documents, so let's talk more about them.

## Views

**Views** are what CouchDB gives us to index, query, and report on our database's documents. If you are reading this book after a MySQL experience, then views will be the replacement for the typical SQL `SELECT` statements.

Now that you have a bit of a background on what views are, you'll notice that in the previous design document, we've created a view called `test`.

## Map functions

Inside the `example` key, we've placed a function called `map`. Map functions are JavaScript functions that consume documents, and then transform them from their original structure into a new key/value pair that your application can then use. Map functions are critical to understand. So, let's look at the simplest implementation of a `map` function to make sure we're all on the same page:

```
"example" : {
    "map" : "function(doc){ emit(doc._id, doc)}"
  }
```

When the example `map` function is called, CouchDB will attempt to index each of the documents in the database and push them through this function in a JSON format using the `doc` argument. From there, we are calling a function called `emit` which accepts a key and a value, from which the key and value will be saved to an array, which will be returned once the indexing is complete.

The key and value of the `emit` function can be whatever field of a document that you would like. In this example, we are passing `doc._id` as the key and `doc` as the value into the `emit` function. `doc._id`, as you might have guessed, is the `_id` field of the document that is being indexed, and `doc` is the entire document represented in a JSON format.

We're going to use views to play with our data in the next section. To make sure that you can completely decipher what views do to our data, make sure that you have at least five or six posts created in the `verge` database.

# Time for action – creating a temporary view

CouchDB provides temporary views for us to use when we are developing or trying to test the result of a view. Let's create a temporary view using Futon so that we can play with some of our data.

1.  Open your browser, and go to Futon (`http://localhost:5984/_utils/`).

2.  Make sure that you are logged in to the `admin` account by checking the bottom of the right column.

3.  Go into our `verge` database by clicking on `verge`.

4.  Click on the drop-down box, and select **Temporary view...**.

5. This form will allow us to play around with views and test them against data in real time.

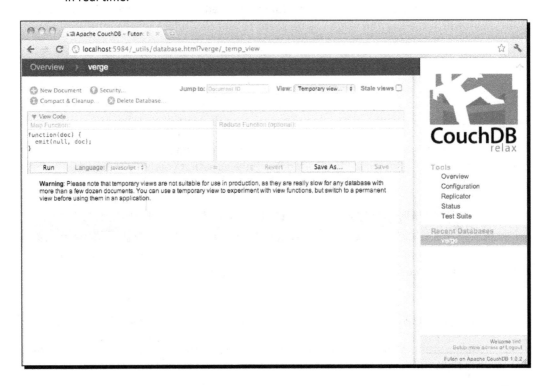

6. Let's edit the code in the **Map Function** text area, so that it matches the example code we looked at earlier:

```
function(doc) {
  emit(doc._id, doc)
}
```

**7.** Click on **Run** to see the results of the `map` function.

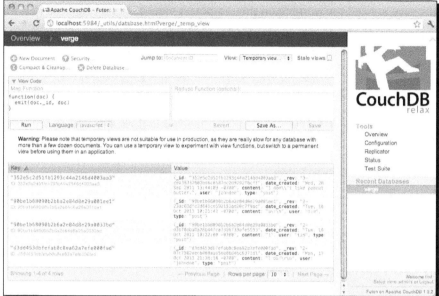

**8.** Let's make sure we're only seeing posts by checking that `doc.type` is equal to `post`:

```
function(doc) {
    if (doc.type == 'post') {
     emit(doc._id, doc);
    }
}
```

**9.** Click on **Run** again, and you'll see the same results.

## What just happened?

We just learned how to create a temporary view in CouchDB so that we can test the `map` function that we looked at earlier. Using the temporary view interface that Futon gives us, we ran our example `map` function and were shown a list of key/value pairs.

Finally, we strengthened our `map` function a bit to make sure that we were only looking at documents with `type` equal to `post`. Right now, the change didn't do anything to our `map` function, but that would change as soon as we added a document with a different type. If you remember, this is because CouchDB stores documents in a flat data store; meaning that as we add new document types, we'll want to be specific on which ones we deal with. So, by adding the `if` statement into our code, we're telling CouchDB to ignore the documents that do not have `type` set as `post`.

## Time for action – creating a view for listing posts

You might have noticed the warning on the temporary view page that said the following:

```
Warning: Please note that temporary views that we'll create are not
suitable for use in production and will respond much slower as your
data increases. It's recommended that you use temporary views in
experimentation and development, but switch to a permanent view before
using them in an application.
```

Let's heed this warning and create a design document so that we can start to build this all into our application.

1. Open your browser to Futon.

2. Navigate to the temporary view page that we were working with:
   (`http://localhost:5984/_utils/database.html?verge/_temp_view`).

3. Let's make our function a bit more useful, and change our key to `doc.user`.

   ```
   function(doc) {
     if (doc.type == 'post') {
      emit(doc.user, doc);
     }
   }
   ```

4. Click on **Run** to see the results.

**5.** Now that our view has the code that we want to use in our application, click on **Save As...** to save this view and create a design document for us.

**6.** A window will be displayed asking us to give the design document and the view a name. Enter _design/application as the name for **Design Document** name and posts_by_user as for **View Name**, then click on **Save**.

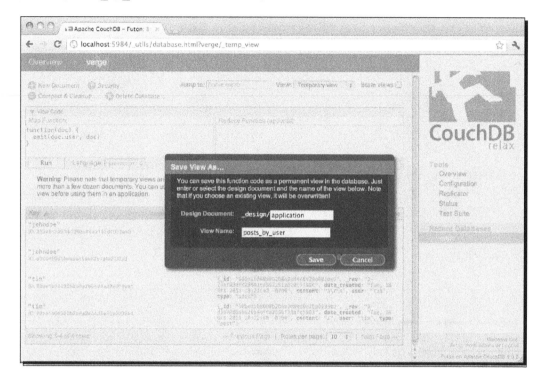

## What just happened?

We created a design document from our temporary view so that our application could use it. This time, we changed the key from doc._id to doc.user, to allow us to select documents with a specific username, which will be helpful in just a few minutes. We then saved this temporary view into a view called, posts_by_user, and saved it into a new design document called _design/application.

You can use Futon's interface to easily check that our design document was created successfully.

1. Open your browser, and go to the verge database in Futon (http://localhost:5984/_utils/database.html?verge).

2. Click on the view drop-down box, and select **Design documents**.

3. You'll only see one document here, which is our newly created design document called `_design/application`.

4. Click on the document, and you'll see the full design document.

While we're at it, let's quickly look at how you can use Futon to test out a design document and its views:

1. Open up your browser to Futon, and make sure you are looking at the `verge` database (`http://localhost:5984/_utils/database.html?verge`).

2. Click on the view drop-down box, and you'll see the application (the name of our design document). Click on the view called `posts_by_user`.

3. You'll be shown the results of the view, as well as the code that is currently associated with it.

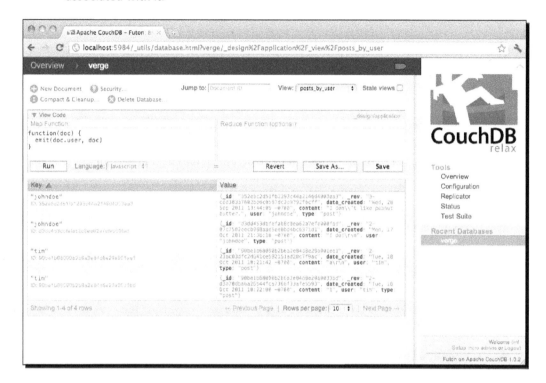

From this page, you can click on the results and see the document details. You can even change the code for your view by simply typing the new code in and clicking on **Save**.

It's been fun playing with these simple views, but let's get a bit deeper into how we can actually use these views to query our documents.

## Querying map functions

There are a variety of options that we can use in our map queries. I will touch on the most common ones, but you can find more my looking at CouchDB's wiki: http://wiki. apache.org/couchdb/HTTP_view_API#Querying_Options.

The most common query options are:

- reduce
- startkey
- endkey
- key

- ◆ `limit`
- ◆ `skip`
- ◆ `descending`
- ◆ `include_docs`

Let's use some of these options with our `posts_by_user` view to see what kind of results we can get.

## Time for action – querying the posts_by_user view

Remember that design document is still a document, which means that we can query it just as we would query a regular document. The only difference will be that we need to use a slightly different URL pattern to hit the correct file.

**1.** Open Terminal.

**2.** Use a `curl` statement to query our design document by passing a key of `johndoe` (or another user in your database that has a decent amount of posts), then pass it through `python -mjson.tool` to make it a bit prettier:

```
curl http://127.0.0.1:5984/verge/_design/application/_view/posts_
by_user?key=%22johndoe%22 | python -mjson.tool
```

**3.** The terminal will respond with something similar to the following:

```
{
    "offset": 0,
    "rows": [
        {
            "id": "352e5c2d51fb1293c44a2146d4003aa3",
            "key": "johndoe",
            "value": {
                "_id": "352e5c2d51fb1293c44a2146d4003aa3",
                "_rev": "3-ced38337602bd6c0587dc2d9792f6cff",
                "content": "I don\\'t like peanut butter.",
                "date_created": "Wed, 28 Sep 2011 13:44:09 -0700",
                "type": "post",
                "user": "johndoe"
            }
        },
        {
            "id": "d3dd453dbfefab8c8ea62a7efe000fad",
            "key": "johndoe",
            "value": {
```

```
        "_id": "d3dd453dbfefab8c8ea62a7efe000fad",
        "_rev": "2-07c7502eecb088aad5ee8bd4bc6371d1",
        "content": "I do!\r\n",
        "date_created": "Mon, 17 Oct 2011 21:36:18 -0700",
        "type": "post",
        "user": "johndoe"
      }
    }
  ],
  "total_rows": 4
}
```

## What just happened?

We just used a `curl` statement to query the `posts_by_user` view in our application design document. We passed `johndoe` as the key for our view to search with, which CouchDB used to return only documents that matched that key. We then used `python -mjson.tool` so that we could see our output in a friendly manner.

Let's have some more fun and talk through a few quick scenarios to determine how we could solve them with the map's `query` options.

1. What if you really wanted to only retrieve the first post that our `map` function would return for `johndoe`? You can do this by adding `limit=1` to the end of our query string:

   ```
   curl 'http://127.0.0.1:5984/verge/_design/application/_view/posts_
   by_user?key=%22johndoe%22&limit=1' | python -mjson.tool
   ```

2. Your terminal will respond with the following output. Notice that this time you are only getting one post in return:

   ```
   {
       "offset": 0,
       "rows": [
           {
               "id": "352e5c2d51fb1293c44a2146d4003aa3",
               "key": "johndoe",
               "value": {
                   "_id": "352e5c2d51fb1293c44a2146d4003aa3",
                   "_rev": "3-ced38337602bd6c0587dc2d9792f6cff",
                   "content": "I don\\'t like peanut butter.",
                   "date_created": "Wed, 28 Sep 2011 13:44:09 -0700",
                   "type": "post",
                   "user": "johndoe"
   ```

```
                }
            }
        ],
        "total_rows": 4
}
```

3.  Now, what if we wanted to see the last post that our map function would return for `johndoe`? You can do this by adding `descending=true`, along with `limit=1`, to the end of our statement to get the newest one, as follows:

```
curl 'http://127.0.0.1:5984/verge/_design/application/_view/posts_
by_user?key=%22johndoe%22&limit=1&descending=true'| python -mjson.
tool
```

4.  Your command-line will return precisely what you are looking for: the last post created by `johndoe`.

```
{
    "offset": 2,
    "rows": [
        {
            "id": "d3dd453dbfefab8c8ea62a7efe000fad",
            "key": "johndoe",
            "value": {
                "_id": "d3dd453dbfefab8c8ea62a7efe000fad",
                "_rev": "2-07c7502eecb088aad5ee8bd4bc6371d1",
                "content": "I do!\r\n",
                "date_created": "Mon, 17 Oct 2011 21:36:18 -0700",
                "type": "post",
                "user": "johndoe"
            }
        }
    ],
    "total_rows": 4
}
```

With some of those examples under your belt, it should be clear that we can chain and combine our `query` options to retrieve the data in a variety of ways. We could play with querying views for a while, but let's move on to trying to build the `posts_by_user` view into our application, in order to allow us to show a user's posts on their profile.

## Using the view in our application

We've done most of the heavy lifting needed to query our database; we just need to add a few lines of code to our application.

# Time for action – adding support to get_posts_by_user in the post class

1. Open classes/post.php in your text editor.

2. Create a new public function called get_posts_by_user that will accept $username as a parameter.

```
public function get_posts_by_user($username) {

}
```

3. Now, let's create a new instance of Bones, so that we can query CouchDB. Let's also instantiate an array called $posts, which we'll return at the end of this function.

```
public function get_posts_by_user($username) {
  $bones = new Bones();
  $posts = array();


  return $posts;
}
```

4. Next, let's query our view by passing $username as the key, and let's use a foreach function to iterate through all of the results into a holding $_post variable.

```
public function get_posts_by_user($username) {
  $bones = new Bones();
  $posts = array();

  foreach ($bones->couch-
    >get('_design/application/_view/posts_by_user?key="' .
    $username . '"&descending=true')->body->rows as $_post) {

  }

  return $posts;
}
```

5. Finally, let's use the data in the $_post variable to create and populate a new instance of Post. Then, let's add $post to the $posts array.

```
public function get_posts_by_user($username) {
  $bones = new Bones();
  $posts = array();
```

```
    foreach ($bones->couch-
      >get('_design/application/_view/posts_by_user?key="' .
      $username . '"')->body->rows as $_post) {
      $post = new Post();
      $post->_id = $_post->id;
      $post->date_created = $_post->value->date_created;
      $post->content = $_post->value->content;
      $post->user = $_post->value->user;

      array_push($posts, $post);
  }

    return $posts;
  }
```

## What just happened?

We created a function called get_posts_by_user and placed it in our Post class. This function accepted an argument called $username. The get_posts_by_user function uses the get_posts_by_user view to return a list of posts into a generic class, from which we iterated through each document, created individual Post objects, and pushed them into an array. You'll notice that we had to use $_post->value to get the post document. Remember that this is because our view returns a list of keys and values, one for each document, and our entire document lives in the value field.

In short, this function enabled us to pass in a user's username and retrieve an array of posts created by the passed user.

## Time for action – adding posts to the user profile

Now that we have done all of the heavy lifting to get our user's posts, we just have a few more lines of code until we can have them show up in the user profile. Let's start by adding some code in our index.php file to accept the username from the route, pass it to the get_posts_by_user function, and pass the data to the profile view:

*1.* Open index.php, find the /user/:username route, and add the following code to pass the returned posts from our get_posts_by_user function to a variable for our view to access:

```
get('/user/:username', function($app) {
  $app->set('user', User::find_by_username($app-
    >request('username')));

  $app->set('is_current_user', ($app->request('username') ==
    User::current_user() ? true : false));
```

```
$app->set('posts', Post::get_posts_by_user($app-
  >request('username')));

$app->render('user/profile');
});
```

2.  Open `views/user/profile.php`, and add the following code right below the
    **Create a new post** text area so that we can display a list of posts on the user profile
    page:

    ```
    <h2>Posts</h2>
    ```

    ```
    <?php foreach ($posts as $post): ?>
    <div class="post-item row">
      <div class="span7">
        <strong><?php echo $user->name; ?></strong>
        <p>
          <?php echo $post->content; ?>
        </p>
        <?php echo $post->date_created; ?>
      </div>
      <div class="span1">
        <a href=#>(Delete)</a>
      </div>
      <div class="span8"></div>
    </div>
    <?php endforeach; ?>
    ```

3.  Finally, to support some of the new code that we added, let's update our `public/
    css/master.css` file for the profile to look nice and clean.

    ```
    .post-item {padding: 10px 0 10px 0;}
    .post-item .span8 {margin-top: 20px; border-bottom: 1px solid
    #ccc;}
    .post-item .span1 a {color:red;}
    ```

## What just happened?

We just added some code to the `index.php` file so that when users navigate to a user's
profile, our application will take the username from the route to the `get_posts_by_user`
function and pass the result of that function into a variable called `posts`. Then, in the
`views/user/profile.php` page, we looped through the posts and used Bootstraps CSS
rules to make it look nice. Finally, we added a few lines of code to our `master.css` file to
make everything look nice.

In this section, we also added a (`Delete`) link next to each post that doesn't currently do anything. We'll hook this up later in this chapter.

Fire up our browser, and let's check to make sure that everything is working correctly.

1. Open your browser, and log in as one of your users.

2. Click on **My Profile** to see the user profile.

3. You should now see the complete profile with all of the user's posts.

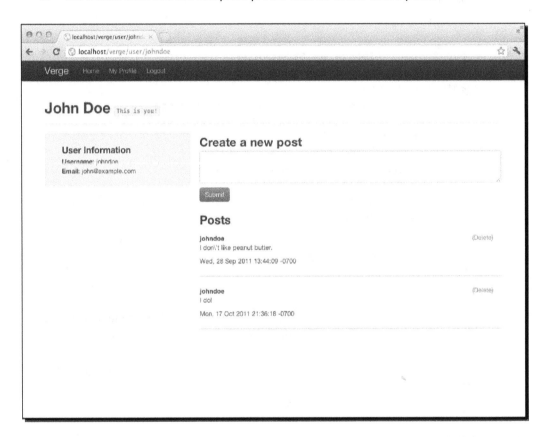

4. Let's test to make sure that our list is working by typing some text into the text area and clicking on **Submit**.

5. Your profile was refreshed, and your new post should show up at the top of the list.

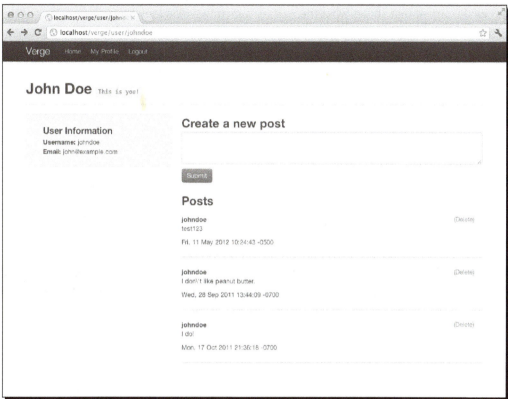

Feel free to pause here, log in as a few different users, and create a ton of posts!

When you're done, let's move on to talk about the map function's companion: **reduce**.

## Reduce functions

**Reduce** allows you to process the key/value pairs returned by the map function, and then break them down into a single value or smaller grouping of values. To make things easier for us, CouchDB comes with three built-in reduce functions called _count, _sum, and _stats.

- _count: It returns the number of mapped values
- _sum: It returns the sum of the mapped values
- _stats: It returns numerical statistics of the mapped values, including sum, count, min, and max

Since reduce functions may not be 100 percent straightforward to a new developer, let's cut to the chase and use one in our application.

In the next section, we are going to create a `reduce` function for our `get_posts_by_user` view that will display the number of posts each user has created. Have a look at our existing design document that shows what the `reduce` function would look like:

```
{
    "_id": "_design/application",
    "_rev": "3-71c0b0bd73a9c9a45ea738f1e9612798",
    "language": "javascript",
    "views": {
        "posts_by_user": {
            "map": "function(doc) {emit(doc.user, doc)}",
            "reduce": "_count"
        }
    }
}
```

In this example, the `reduce` function grouped together all of the usernames from the `map` function and returned a count of how many times each username occurred in the list.

## Time for action – creating the reduce function in Futon

Adding a `reduce` function to a view is surprisingly easy to do using Futon.

1.  Open your browser and go to the `verge` database in Futon (`http://localhost:5984/_utils/database.html?verge`).

2.  Click on the view drop-down box, and you'll see the application (the name of our design document). You can click on the view called `posts_by_user`.

3.  Click on **View Code**, so that you can see the text areas for **Map** and **Reduce**.

4.  Enter `_count` into the **Reduce** text area, and click on **Save**.

5.  You can verify that your `reduce` function is working properly by clicking on the **Reduce** checkbox right below the **Save** button.

**6.** You should see a screenshot similar to the following:

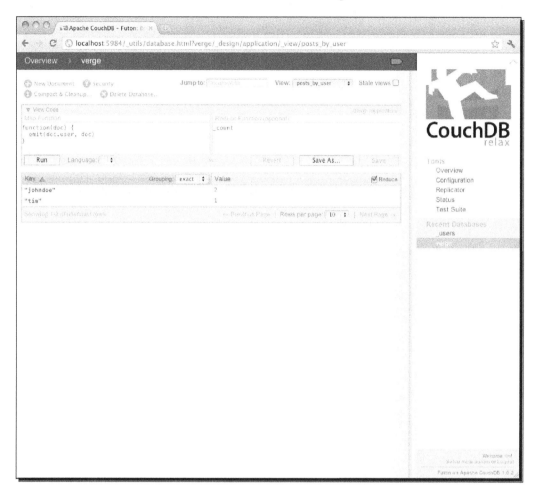

## *What just happened?*

We just used Futon to update our view to use a `_count reduce` function. We then tested the `reduce` function in the same view by clicking on the **Reduce** checkbox. You'll notice that our `reduce` function also returned a key/value pair with the key equal to the username and the value equal to the count of posts that they have created.

# Time for action – adding support to our application to consume the reduce function

Now that we have created the reduce function, let's add some code to our application to retrieve the value.

1. Open classes/post.php.

2. Now that we've created a reduce function, we need to make sure that the get_posts_by_user function uses the view without using the reduce function. We'll do this by adding reduce=false to the query string. This tells the view not to run the reduce function.

```
public function get_posts_by_user($username) {
  $bones = new Bones();
  $posts = array();

  foreach ($bones->couch-
    >get('_design/application/_view/posts_by_user?key="' .
    $username . '"&descending=true&reduce=false')->body->rows as
    $_post) {
```

3. Create a new public function called get_post_count_by_user that will accept $username as a parameter.

```
public function get_post_count_by_user($username) {

}
```

4. Let's add a call to our view that mimics our get_posts_by_user function. But, this time, we'll add reduce=true to the query string. Once we get a result from the view, traverse through the data to get the value that is located in the value of the first returned row.

```
public function get_post_count_by_user($username) {
  $bones = new Bones();

  $rows = $bones->couch-
    >get('_design/application/_view/posts_by_user?key="' . "
    $username . '"&reduce=true')->body->rows;

  if ($rows) {
    return $rows[0]->value;
  } else {
    return 0;
  }
}
```

**5.** Open `index.php`, and find the `/user/:username` route.

**6.** Add code to pass the value from the `get_post_count_by_user` function to a variable that our view can access.

```
get('/user/:username', function($app) {
    $app->set('user', User::get_by_username($app-
        >request('username')));

    $app->set('is_current_user', ($app->request('username') ==
        User::current_user() ? true : false));

    $app->set('posts', Post::get_posts_by_user($app-
        >request('username')));

    $app->set('post_count', Post::get_post_count_by_user($app-
        >request('username')));

    $app->render('user/profile');
});
```

**7.** Finally, open up the user profile (`views/user/profile.php`) and display the `$post_count` variable at the top of our post list.

```
<h2>Posts (<?php echo $post_count; ?>)</h2>
```

## What just happened?

We started this section by updating our existing `get_posts_by_user` function and told it not to run the `reduce` function, just the `map` function. Then, we created a function called `get_post_count_by_user` that accessed our `posts_by_user` view. But, this time, we told it to run the `reduce` function by passing `reduce=true` in our call. When we received the value from the `reduce` function, we navigated into the value of the first row and returned it. We're looking at just one row, because we're only passing in one username, meaning that only one value will be returned.

We then called `get_post_count_by_user` from the user profile route and passed it to the `user/profile.php` view. In the view, we outputted `$post_count` at the top of the list of posts.

With that small amount of code, we've added a cool piece of functionality to our profile. Let's test it out to see what `$post_count` displays.

1. Open your browser, and go to John Doe's user profile by going to:
   `http://localhost/verge/user/johndoe`.

2. Notice that we are now displaying the number of posts at the top of the `post` list.

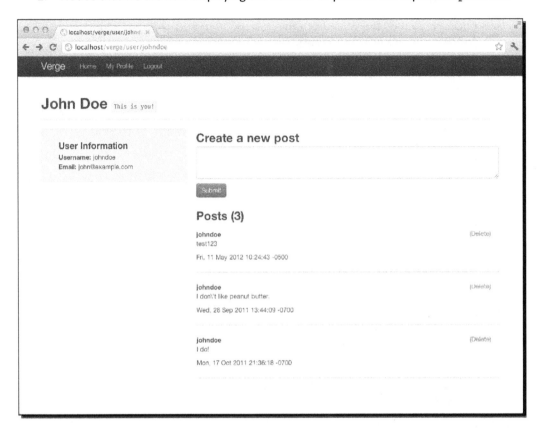

## More with MapReduce

Using the `map` and `reduce` functions together is often referred to as **MapReduce**, and when used together they can be a powerful method of data analysis. Unfortunately, we can't go through a variety of case studies in this book, but I'll include some references for further education at the end of this chapter.

# Validation

In this section, we're going to expose and talk about another really unique property of CouchDB – its built-in support for document function. This feature allows us to have tighter controls on our data and can safeguard us from some nasty problems that can occur with web applications.

Remember that our `verge` database is readable by any user, which hasn't really been a problem for us yet. But, what if, for instance, someone found out where our database was stored? They could easily create and delete the documents in our database in no time.

In order to fully illustrate this problem, let's add a functionality that will allow our users to delete their posts. This simple function will illustrate a potential security hole, which we will then patch up with CouchDB's `validation` function.

## Time for action – adding support for $_rev to our classes

Up until this point, we've seen the `_rev` key in our CouchDB documents, but we haven't had to actually use it in our application. In order for us to take any actions on an already existing document, we'll need to pass `_rev`, along with `_id`, to ensure that we are acting on the most recent document.

Let's prepare for this by adding a `$_rev` variable to our `base` class.

1. Open `classes/base.php` in your working directory, and add the `$_rev` variable.

```
abstract class Base
{
  protected $_id;
  protected $_rev;
  protected $type;
```

2. Unfortunately, now anytime we call the `to_json` function, `_rev` will always be included, regardless of it being used or not. If we were to send CouchDB a `null` `_rev`, it would throw an error. So, let's add some code to the `to_json` function in `classes/base.php` to unset our `_rev` variable if it has no value set.

```
public function to_json() {
  if (isset($this->_rev) === false) {
    unset($this->_rev);
  }

  return json_encode(get_object_vars($this));
}
```

## What just happened?

We added `$_rev` to our `base` class. Up until this point, we haven't really had a need to use this value, but it's a requirement when we are dealing with existing documents. After adding `$_rev` to the base class, we had to retrofit our `to_json` function so that it would unset `$_rev` if it didn't have a value set.

# Time for action – adding support to delete posts in our application

Now that we have access to the _rev variable in our base class, let's add support so that our application can delete posts from the user profile.

1. Let's start by opening classes/post.php and adding a line of code to the get_posts_by_user function so that we have _rev available to us.

```
public function get_posts_by_user($username) {
  $bones = new Bones();
  $posts = array();

  foreach $bones->couch-
    >get('_design/application/_view/posts_by_user?key="' .
    $username . '"&descending=true&reduce=false')->body->rows as
    $_post) {

    $post = new Post();
    $post->_id = $_post->value->_id;
    $post->_rev = $_post->value->_rev;
    $post->date_created = $_post->value->date_created;
```

2. Next, let's create a nice and simple delete function in the classes/post.php file, so we can delete the posts.

```
public function delete() {
  $bones = new Bones();

  try {
    $bones->couch->delete($this->_id, $this->_rev);
  }
  catch(SagCouchException $e) {
    $bones->error500($e);
  }
}
```

3. Now that we have the backend support to delete the posts, let's add a route in our index.php file that accepts _id and _rev. With this route, we can trigger the deletion of posts from our profile page.

```
get('/post/delete/:id/:rev', function($app) {
  $post = new Post();
  $post->_id = $app->request('id');
  $post->_rev = $app->request('rev'
```

```php
            $post->delete();

            $app->set('success', 'Your post has been deleted');
            $app->redirect('/user/' . User::current_user());
        });
```

**4.** Finally, let's update our views/user/profile.php page, so that when users click on the delete link, they hit our route, and we pass the necessary variables.

```php
<?php foreach ($posts as $post): ?>
    <div class="post-item row">
        <div class="span7">
            <strong><?php echo $user->name; ?></strong>
            <p>
                <?php echo $post->content; ?>
            </p>
            <?php echo $post->date_created; ?>
        </div>
        <div class="span1">
            <a href="<?php echo $this->make_route('/post/delete/' .
              $post->_id . '/' . $post->_rev)?>" class="delete">
                (Delete)
            </a>
        </div>
        <div class="span8"></div>
    </div>
<?php endforeach; ?>
```

## What just happened?

We just added support for users to delete posts from their profile. We started by making sure that we returned _rev to our post objects in the get_posts_by_user function, so that we can pass it when we are attempting to delete a post. Next, we created a delete function in our post class that accepts $id and $rev as attributes and calls Sag's delete method. Then, we created a new route called /post/delete that allows us to pass _id and _rev to it. In this route, we created a new Post object to which we set _id and _rev and then called the delete function. We then set the success variable and refreshed the profile.

Finally, we made the delete link operational in the user profile by passing $post->_id and $post->_rev to the /post/delete route.

Sweet! We can now click on **Delete** next to any post on the site, and it will be removed from the database. Let's give it a shot.

1. Open your browser and go to `http://localhost/verge`.
2. Log in as any user, and go to their user profile.
3. Click on the **(Delete)** button.
4. The page will reload, and your post will be magically gone!

This code technically works just as we planned, but if you played around with deleting posts for a few minutes, you might have noticed that we have a problem here. Right now, any user can delete a post from any profile, meaning that I could go to your profile and delete all of your posts. Of course, we can quickly fix this problem by hiding the **Delete** button. But, let's take a step back, and quickly think about this.

What would happen if someone came across (or guessed) the `_id` and `_rev` of a user's posts, and passed it to the `/post/delete` route? The post would be deleted, because we don't have any user-level validation to ensure that the person trying to delete the document is actually the owner of the document.

Let's fix this problem on a database level first, then we'll work backwards and hide the **Delete** button correctly in the interface.

## CouchDB's support for validation

CouchDB provides validation for documents via a function in the design document called `validate_doc_update`. This function can cancel the creation/update/deletion of a document if the action doesn't meet our criteria. Validation functions have a defined structure and fit right into a design document as follows:

```
{
  "_id": "_design/application",
  "_rev": "3-71c0b0bd73a9c9a45ea738f1e9612798",
  "language": "javascript",
  "validate_doc_update": "function(newDoc, oldDoc, userCtx)          {
    //JavaScript Code }",
  "views": {
    "posts_by_user": {
      "map": "function(doc) {emit(doc.user, doc)}",
      "reduce": "_count"
    }
  }
}
```

Let's look at the `validate_doc_update` function and make sure we are clear on what is happening here.

```
function(newDoc, oldDoc, userCtx) {   //JavaScript Code }
```

- ◆  `newDoc`: It is the document that you are trying to save
- ◆  `oldDoc`: It is the existing document (if there is an existing one)
- ◆  `userCtx`: It is the user object and their roles

Now that we know what parameters we have at our disposal, let's make a simple `validate` function that ensures that only the creator of a document can update or delete that document.

## Time for action – adding a validate function to ensure that only creators can update or delete their documents

Adding `validate` functions can be a bit odd, because unlike views, there isn't a nice interface in Futon for us to use. The quickest way to add the `validate_doc_update` function is to treat it like a normal field in our document and type the code right into the value. It's a bit strange, but it is the quickest way to adjust design documents. At the end of the chapter, I'll give you some resources if you want to get a bit cleaner with how you manage design documents.

1.  Open your browser and go to Futon (`http://localhost:5984/_utils/`).

2.  Make sure that you are logged in to the `admin` account by checking that the bottom right column says **Welcome**.

3.  Go to our `verge` database by clicking on `verge`.

4.  Click on our `_design/application` design document.

5.  Click on **Add Field**, and call this field `validate_doc_update`.

6.  In the **Value** text area, add the following code (formatting and indents don't matter):
```
function(newDoc, oldDoc, userCtx) {
  if (newDoc.user) {
    if(newDoc.user != userCtx.name) {
      throw({"forbidden": "You may only update this document with
        user " + userCtx.name});
    }
  }
}
```

7.  Click on **Save**, and your document will be updated to include the validate function.

## What just happened?

We just used Futon to update our _design/application design document. We used the simple interface to create the validate_doc_update function and put our validation code in the value. The code might look a bit confusing; let's walk through it real quick.

1. First, we checked to make sure that the document we're saving has a user variable attached to it using this if statement:

   ```
   if (newDoc.user).
   ```

2. Then, we checked to see if the username on the document matched that of the currently logged-in user:

   ```
   if(newDoc.user != userCtx.name).
   ```

3. If it turns out that the document did have a user tied to it, and the user that attempted to save was not the logged-in user, then we throw a forbidden error (HTTP response with status code 403) with details on why the document could not be saved with this line of code:

   ```
   throw({"forbidden": "You may only update this document with user "
   + userCtx.name});
   ```

It's worth noting that a design document can only have one validate_doc_update function. So, if you want to carry out different types of validations on different documents, then you would have to do something as follows:

```
function(newDoc, oldDoc, userCtx) {
  if (newDoc.type == "post") {
    // validation logic for posts
  }
  if (newDoc.type == "comment") {
    // validation logic for comments
  }
}
```

There is a lot more we could do with validation functions. In fact, the _users database, which we use frequently, drives all of the user validation and controls using the validate_doc_update function.

Now, let's test out our validation function.

1. Open your browser, and go to http://localhost/verge.

2. Log in as a different user than John Doe.

3. Go to the profile of John Doe by going to:
   http://localhost/verge/user/johndoe.

4. Try clicking on the (Delete) button.

5. Your browser will display the following message to you:

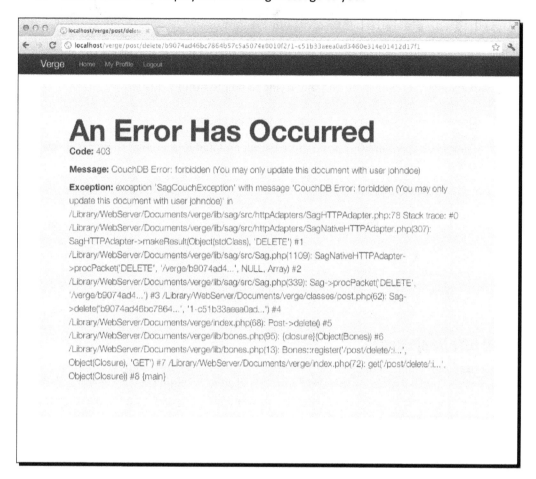

Great! CouchDB threw a 403 error for us, because it knew that we weren't logged in as John Doe and we tried to delete one of his posts. If you wanted to investigate further, you could log in as John Doe again and verify that you can delete his posts when you are logged in as him.

We can feel safe in knowing that no matter what interface a user uses, Sag, curl, or even through Futon, CouchDB will ensure that a user must own a document in order for them to delete it.

We could add a more graceful error message for this validation error, but it's rare that this error will happen, so let's move on for now. Let's just add some simple logic to our user profile so users don't have the ability to delete the posts of other users.

## Time for action – hiding the delete buttons when not on the current user's profile

Hiding the delete buttons from a user is actually very easy for us to do. While this method is no replacement for our previous validation function, it's a nice and friendly way for us to safeguard against users from accidentally trying to delete other's posts.

1. Open `view/user/profile.php` in your text editor.

2. Find the loop where our posts are created, and add this code around our delete button.

```
<div class="span1">
  <?php if ($is_current_user) { ?>
    <a href="<?php echo $this->make_route('/post/delete/' . $post-
>
      _id . '/' . $post->_rev)?>" class="delete">(Delete)
    </a>
  <?php } ?>
</div>
```

### What just happened?

We just used our simple variable `$is_current_user` to hide the delete button from a user when they are looking at someone else's profile and show it when they are looking at their own. This is the same technique we used to show and hide the text area for creating posts earlier in this chapter.

If one of your users went to another user's profile now, they wouldn't be able to see the option to delete one of their posts. Even if they somehow managed to find out the `_id` and `_rev` of a post, and were able to trigger the deletion of a post, the `validation` function would stop them dead in their tracks.

## Wrapping up

We went through a lot in this chapter, but I was only able to touch on a few points that would definitely be worth researching more.

# Want more examples?

Learning advanced techniques for `MapReduce` functions and design documents could take up an entire book. In fact, there is an entire book on it! If you want to learn more about real use-case scenarios and how to deal with one-to-many and many-to-many relationships, then check out a book from *Bradley Holt* called *Writing and Querying MapReduce Views in CouchDB*.

# Working with design documents in Futon is too hard!

You aren't the only one who thinks that working with design documents in Futon is too hard. There are a few tools that might be worth checking out:

- **CouchApp** (`http://couchapp.org/`): It is a utility that can enable you to create full-blown JavaScript applications that run inside of CouchDB. However, the way it manages design documents can also make your life easier when developing PHP applications.

- **LoveSeat** (`http://www.russiantequila.com/wordpress/?p=119`): It is a lightweight editor that works under Mono, meaning it will work on any operating system. It allows you to very easily manage your documents and design documents.

# Summary

In this chapter, we took a deep dive into CouchDB and utilized some of its unique characteristics to make our apps simpler. More specifically, we talked about design documents and how CouchDB uses them, creating views and a design document using Futon. We learned about views, how we can query them with options, such as SQL, queried our posts in views with the help of `MapReduce`, consumed a view in our application to dynamically display a list and count of posts for each user, and we also learned how to build validation into CouchDB and used it to safeguard our application.

In the next chapter, we will take our application a few steps further and add fun features, such as improving our user experience with JQuery, adding pagination, using Gravatars, and more!

# 9
# Adding Bells and Whistles to your Application

*We've added a lot of solid functionality to our application. However, there are a few missing features that some people might consider "nice to have" and are important to us so that our application has a nice user experience.*

In this chapter, we will:

- Add jQuery to the project and use it to simplify the delete buttons
- Add basic pagination to user posts by using CouchDB views and jQuery
- Add profile images for all of our users using Gravatar's web service

These features are fun, little additions, and they will also open your eyes to what's possible when you combine other libraries with CouchDB and PHP.

## Adding jQuery to our project

Even though this book is primarily about writing applications in PHP, JavaScript has turned into an almost essential tool in a developer's tool belt when building great applications. We've already used JavaScript in our CouchDB views but, in this chapter, we'll use JavaScript for its most common use case—improving our user experience. In order for us to write simpler JavaScript, we're going to use a popular library called **jQuery**. If you haven't used jQuery before, you are going to be pleasantly surprised at how much it simplifies both common and complex operations in JavaScript.

# Installing jQuery

Luckily, jQuery is incredibly simple to get into any project. We could download it from `http://www.jquery.com`, but, because we want to focus on speed, we can actually use it without installing anything into our repository.

## Time for action – adding jQuery to our project

Because of the influx of people using jQuery, Google has set up a content delivery network that serves up the jQuery library for us without anything being required in our project. Let's tell our `layout.php` file where to find jQuery.

Open the `layout.php` file, and add the following code right before the end of the body section:

```
<script type="text/javascript" src=
  "//ajax.googleapis.com/ajax/libs/jquery/1.7.2/jquery.min.js">
</script>
</body>
</html>
```

## What just happened?

We just added one line of code before the end of our body tag in the `layout.php` file. That's all it took to use jQuery with our project! You may be wondering why we decided to put our jQuery library all the way at the bottom of our file. The simplest explanation is that as a browser loads code, it does so one line at a time. By putting JavaScript at the bottom of the page, it allows the other elements, such as CSS and HTML markup, to load faster, giving the user the impression that things are loading fast.

## Time for action – creating master.js and connecting Boostrap's JavaScript files

As our application grows, we'll want to be able to add our JavaScript into external files. Let's create a file called `master.js` that will hold all of our application's JavaScript and then connect Bootstrap's JavaScript files that we downloaded in *Chapter 6, Modeling Users*.

1. Create a new file called `master.js` in the `public/js` folder.

2. Open the `layout.php` file, and add the following code right before the end of the body section:

```
<script type="text/javascript" src=
  "//ajax.googleapis.com/ajax/libs/jquery
  /1.7.2/jquery.min.js">
```

```
    </script>

    <script type="text/javascript" src="<?php echo $this-
      >make_route('/js/bootstrap.min.js') ?>">
    </script>

    <script type="text/javascript" src="<?php echo $this-
      >make_route('/js/master.js') ?>">
    </script>

  </body>
</html>
```

## What just happened?

We created a blank file called `master.js`, which is where all of our application's JavaScript will be live. Next, we adjusted our `layout.php` file again, allowing us to include the `boostrap.min.js` file that we downloaded in *Chapter 6*, as well as our newly created `master.js` file.

 When it comes to writing JavaScript, the order in which you load files is important. As we write jQuery later in this chapter, it will be important for our browser to load the jQuery file first, so it knows what jQuery is and how the syntax works.

# Using jQuery to improve our site

Now that we have jQuery, let's jump right into using it to improve our site a little bit. There are a lot of different ways in which you can write the jQuery and JavaScript code, but we're going to stick to the absolute basics in this book and try to keep it simple.

## Fixing our delete post action to actually use HTTP delete

One of the things you might have noticed early in the last chapter is that when we coded the deletion of posts from the user's profile, we actually used the `GET HTTP` method instead of the `DELETE` method. This is because it's difficult to trigger a `DELETE` route without using JavaScript. So, in the following section, we're going to improve the deletion process in order for it to work as follows:

1. A user clicks on **Delete** on a post.
2. A `DELETE AJAX` request is made from jQuery to our application.

3. Our application will delete the post document and report back to jQuery that everything went as expected.

4. The post will fade from the view without our user needing to refresh the page.

This will be a nice improvement to our user profile, because we won't require our page to reload each time an action is performed.

## Time for action – improving our user experience by using AJAX to delete posts

Let's get our feet wet with a bit of jQuery by adding some code to our `master.js` file that will allow us to delete posts using JavaScript. Don't be overwhelmed if the syntax of jQuery isn't familiar to you at first; stick with it, and I think you'll be incredibly pleased with the results.

*1.* Open `public/js/master.js`, and make sure the jQuery code will run when the page is finished loading by adding a `$(document).ready` event to our file. This piece of code means that any JavaScript code inside of this function will be run once the page has finished loading:

```
$(document).ready(function() {

});
```

*2.* Now, let's add an event that binds the `click` event to any button that has the `delete` class in our HTML. All of the code inside the brackets of `function(event)` will be run each time one of our delete post buttons is clicked:

```
$(document).ready(function() {
  $('.delete').bind('click', function(event){

  });
});
```

*3.* Let's prevent the link from taking us to a new page, as it normally does, with a piece of code called `event.preventDefault()`. Then, let's save the `href` attribute of the clicked link into a variable called `location`, so that we can use it in our AJAX call:

```
$(document).ready(function() {
  $('.delete').bind( 'click', function(event){
    event.preventDefault();
    var location = $(this).attr('href');

  });
});
```

**4.** Finally, let's create a basic AJAX request that will call our application and delete the post for us:

```
$(document).ready(function() {
  $('.delete').bind( 'click', function(){
    event.preventDefault();
    var location = $(this).attr('href');
    $.ajax({
      type: 'DELETE',
      url: location,
      context: $(this),
      success: function(){
        $(this).parent().parent().fadeOut();
      },
      error: function (request, status, error) {
        alert('An error occurred, please try again.');
      }
    });

  });
});
```

## What just happened?

We just learned how to make an AJAX request with JavaScript in just a few lines of code. We started by wrapping our code in a $(document).ready function that is run once the page has completely loaded. We then added a function that captures the click of any of our delete post links in our application. Finally, the most complex part of the script is our AJAX call. Let's talk through this a bit so that it makes sense. jQuery has a function called $.ajax that has a variety of options (which are all viewable here: http://api.jquery.com/jQuery.ajax/). Let's walk through each of the options that I've used in the piece of code given previously and make sure you know what they mean.

- type: 'DELETE' means that we want to use the DELETE HTTP method for our request.

- url: location means that we are going to use the href attribute of the clicked link for our request. This will make sure the correct post is deleted.

- context: $(this) is the object that will be used for all AJAX callbacks. So, in this example, all the code that is inside the success option of this call will use the clicked link as the context for all calls.

- ◆ `success: function()` is called whenever our AJAX request is complete. We placed the following code inside this function: `$(this).parent().parent().fadeOut();`. This means that we're going to look two HTML levels up from the clicked link. This means that we're going to look for `<div class="post-item row">` of the post, and we're going to fade it out of view.

- ◆ `error: function (request, status, error)` is run whenever an error occurs in your code. Right now, we're just displaying an alert box, which is not the most elegant approach, especially since we aren't supplying the user with details of what happened. This will work for us for now, but if you want some bonus points, play a bit with this function and see if you can make it a bit more graceful.

Awesome! We just added some code that will really improve the user's experience. As your application grows, and you add more features to it, make sure to keep jQuery's AJAX method in mind, which will definitely make things easier.

## Updating our route to use the DELETE HTTP method

Now that we are correctly using `DELETE` as our `HTTP` method through our AJAX call, we need to update our routes, so our code knows how to handle the route.

1. Open `index.php`, and look for the `post/delete/:id/:rev` route that we created in the previous chapter:

```
get('/post/delete/:id/:rev', function($app) {
  $post = new Post();
  $post->_id = $app->request('id');
  $post->_rev = $app->request('rev');
  $post->delete();

  $app->set('success', 'Your post has been deleted');
  $app->redirect('/user/' . User::current_user());
});
```

2. Let's change the route to use a `delete` method by changing `get` to `delete`. Then, remove the `success` variable and the redirection code, because we'll no longer need them:

```
delete('/post/delete/:id/:rev', function($app) {
  $post = new Post();
  $post->_id = $app->request('id');
  $post->_rev = $app->request('rev');
  $post->delete();
});
```

## Let's test it out!

While testing this feature, make sure to stop and appreciate all of the technologies that are working together in unison to solve a somewhat complex problem.

1. Go to `http://localhost/verge/login`, and log in to the application as `johndoe`.

2. Click on **My Profile**.

3. Click on `(Delete)` next to one of your posts.

4. The deleted posts will fade out of view, and the other posts will bump up on the page.

# Adding simple pagination using jQuery

As our application grows, posts will start to fill up the profile of a user. What happens if our application becomes successful, and people start using it? Hundreds of posts will be printed to the profile view each time the page loads. Something like this could absolutely cripple your application as it starts to grow.

With that in mind, we're going to create some pagination on our profile pages. Our simple pagination system will work as follows:

1. By default, we'll show 10 posts on a page. When a user wants to see more, they'll click on a **Load More** link.

2. When the **Show More** link is clicked, jQuery will figure out how many items to skip and tell Bones which documents to retrieve.

3. Bones will use Sag to call CouchDB and get more posts through the `posts_by_user` view.

4. Bones will load the results into a partial view that contains our HTML layout for how posts need to be formatted. This HTML will be returned to jQuery to display on our page.

There's quite a bit going on there, but this type of feature is a common occurrence in most applications. So, let's jump in and see if we can piece this all together.

# Time for action – taking posts out of profile.php and putting them in their own partial view

The code for listing posts sits directly inside the `profile.php` page, which was fine up until now. However, in a moment, we'll want to be able to display posts via `callback` from Javascript, which on if we're not careful, could mean duplicate code or inconsistent layout. Let's safeguard ourselves against that by moving our code into a partial view that we can reuse easily.

1. Create a new file called _posts.php in views/user.

2. Copy and paste the `foreach` code that lists out posts from `views/user/profile.php`, and paste it into our new file _posts.php. The end result of _posts.php should as follows:

```php
<?php foreach ($posts as $post): ?>
  <div class="post-item row">
    <div class="span7">
      <strong><?php echo $user->name; ?></strong>
      <p>
        <?php echo $post->content; ?>
      </p>
      <?php echo $post->date_created; ?>
    </div>
    <div class="span1">
      <?php if ($is_current_user) { ?>

        <a href="<?php echo $this->make_route('/post/delete/' .
          $post->_id . '/' . $post->_rev)?>" class="delete">
          (Delete)

        </a>
      <?php } ?>
    </div>
    <div class="span8"></div>
  </div>
<?php endforeach; ?>
```

3. Now, let's remove the same `foreach` statement from `views/user/profile.php`, and replace it with an `include` call to the newly created _posts file. Then let's add a `span` inside our list's `h2` element so that we can easily access it via jQuery.

```html
<h2>
  Posts (<span id="post_count"><?php echo $post_count; ?></span>)
</h2>
```

```
<div id="post_list">
  <?php include('_posts.php'); ?>
</div>
```

## What just happened?

We took all of the code that listed the posts out of `profile.php` and moved it into a new partial called `_posts.php`. We began the filename with an underscore for no other reason than for us to tell that it's different than normal views when we are looking through our source code. By partial view, I meant that it's meant to be loaded into another page, by itself, it would probably serve no purpose. On the surface, our application will function exactly the same as it did before we moved our code to a partial view.

We then altered our code in `profile.php`, so that it would make it easier to work with using jQuery. We added a `span` element with an ID of `post_count` inside of our `h2` element. This `span` element just contains the number of total posts. We'll use this soon to tell us if we've loaded all of the posts we needed into our list. We then wrapped our list of posts with a `div` with the ID `post_list`. We're going to use this identifier to append new posts to the list from our pagination control.

## Adding backend support for pagination

We don't need another function for pagination. Let's just improve the `Post` class's `get_posts_by_user` function. All we need to do is add the `skip` and `limit` options, which we will then pass to the `posts_by_user` view in CouchDB. Passing `skip` to this view will enable us to skip a certain number of records in the results that it sends us, and `limit` will allow us to only show a certain number of posts at a time. By combining these two variables, we will have support for pagination!

## Time for action – adjusting our get_posts_by_user function to skip and limit posts

Now that we know what to do, let's jump right into editing our `classes/post.php` file and adjusting our `get_posts_by_user` function so that we can add `$skip` and `$limit` as arguments.

1. Open the `Post` class by opening the file called `classes/post.php`.

2. Find our `get_posts_by_user` function, and add `$skip` with a default value of `0` and `$limit` with a default value of `10`.

```
public function get_posts_by_user($username, $skip = 0,
  $limit = 10) {
  $bones = new Bones();
```

```
$posts = array();

...
}
```

**3.** Update our `get` call to Sag so that it passes the value of `$skip` and `$limit` into the query.

```
public function get_posts_by_user($username, $skip = 0,
  $limit = 10) {
  $bones = new Bones();
  $posts = array();

  foreach ($bones->couch->
    get('_design/application/_view/posts_by_user?key="' .
    $username . '"&descending=true&reduce=false&skip=' . $skip .
    '&limit=' . $limit)->body->rows as $_post) {
  ...

  }
```

**4.** Now that we have updated our function to include `skip` and `limit`, let's create a new route in `index.php` that's similar to the `user/:username` route but takes in a route variable of `skip` to drive the pagination. In this route, we're just going to return _posts partially, instead of the whole layout:

```
get('/user/:username/:skip', function($app) {
  $app->set('user', User::get_by_username($app->
    request('username')));

  $app->set('is_current_user', ($app->request('username') ==
    User::current_user() ? true : false));

  $app->set('posts', Post::get_posts_by_user($app->
    request('username'), $app->request('skip')));

  $app->set('post_count', Post::get_post_count_by_user($app->
    request('username')));

  $app->render('user/_posts', false);
});
```

# What just happened?

We just added additional `$skip` and `$limit` options to the `get_posts_by_user` function. We also set things up so that our current calls will function without changing anything, as we set default values for each variable. Our existing call in the user profile will now also show the first 10 posts.

We then created a new route called `/user/:username/:skip`, where `skip` is the number of items we want to skip when querying. Everything else in this function is exactly the same as in the `/user/:username` route, except for the fact that we are returning the results into our partial and with a layout of `false`, so there's no layout wrapper. We're doing this so that jQuery can call this route, and it will simply return the list of posts it needs to add to the end of the list on the page.

# Let's test it out!

Let's make sure that our `/user/:username/:skip` route works as expected by playing around with it directly through the browser.

1. Go to `http://localhost/verge/user/johndoe/0` (or any user that has a decent number of posts).

2. Your browser will return a big list of posts using `views/user/_posts.php` as a template. Notice that it's showing us 10 total posts, starting with the most recent post.

3. Now, let's try to skip the first 10 posts (as our pager will eventually do) and retrieve the next 10 posts by going to: `http://localhost/verge/user/johndoe/10`

4. Our code hopefully worked great. I only had 12 posts on this account, so this view skipped the first 10 posts and showed the last two.

This all functioned exactly as we were expecting, but there's a little bit of clean-up to be done in our code.

## Time for action – refactoring our code so it's not redundant

Although our code works just fine, you might have noticed that we have near identical code in `/user/:username` and `/user/:username/:skip`. We can cut down on code bloat by moving all of the redundant code into a function and calling it from each route. Let's do this so we can stay in the habit of keeping our code clean.

1. Open `index.php`, and create a function called `get_user_profile` that takes `$app` as a parameter, and place it above `/user/:username` route.

```
function get_user_profile($app) {


}
```

2. Copy the code from `/user/:username/:skip` into this function. But, this time, instead of just passing `$app->request('skip')`, let's check if it exists. If it exists, let's pass it to the `get_posts_by_user` function. If it doesn't exist, we'll just pass it `0`.

```
function get_user_profile($app) {
  $app->set('user', User::get_by_username($app->
    request('username')));
```

```
$app->set('is_current_user', ($app->request('username') ==
  User::current_user() ? true : false));

$app->set('posts', Post::get_posts_by_user($app->
  request('username'), ($app->request('skip') ? $app->
  request('skip') : 0)));

$app->set('post_count', Post::get_post_count_by_user($app->
  request('username')));
}
```

**3.** Finally, let's clean up both of our profile functions so that both of them just call the
get_user_profile function.

```
get('/user/:username', function($app) {
  get_user_profile($app);
  $app->render('user/profile');
});

get('/user/:username/:skip', function($app) {
  get_user_profile($app);
  $app->render('user/_posts', false);
});
```

## What just happened?

We just simplified our user profile routes by moving most of the logic into a new function
called get_user_profile. The only piece of functionality that was different between the
two routes was the request variable skip. So, we put a shorthand if statement in the call
to the function Posts::get_posts_by_user that would pass the skip request variable
if it existed; but if it didn't, we would just pass it 0. Adding this little piece of functionality
allowed us to use the same code for the two different routes. Finally, we plugged our
brand new function into our routes, and were ready to bask in the simplicity of the code.
Everything will still work the same as it did before, but it's much easier to read and will be
easier for us to update in the future.

Refactoring and consistently cleaning up code is an important process to follow as you
develop; you'll thank yourself for doing this later!

## Time for action – adding frontend support for pagination

We almost have complete support for pagination. All we need to do now is add a little bit of HTML and JavaScript to our project, and we'll have a nice experience.

**1.** Let's start by adding a line of CSS into our `master.css` file, so that our **Load More** button will look pretty.

```
#load_more a {padding: 10px 0 10px 0; display: block; text-align:
    center; background: #e4e4e4; cursor: pointer;}
```

**2.** Now that we have the CSS in place, let's add the HTML for our **Load More** button at the bottom of the `post` list inside our `profile.php` view.

```html
<h2>
    Posts (<span id="post_count"><?php echo $post_count; ?></span>)
</h2>
<div id="post_list">
    <?php include('_posts.php'); ?>
</div>
<div id="load_more" class="row">
    <div class="span8">
        <a id="more_posts" href="#">Load More...</a>
    </div>
</div>
```

**3.** Now, let's open `master.js`, and create a function inside the closing brackets of the `$(document).ready` function. This function will target the `click` event of the any element with the ID of `more_posts`.

```javascript
$('#more_posts').bind( 'click', function(event){
    event.preventDefault();

});

});
```

**4.** In order for us to call the `/user/:username/:skip` route, we will need to use a JavaScript function called `window.location.pathname` to grab the current URL of the page. Then, we'll append the number of post items at the end of the string so that we skip the number of posts that are currently displayed on the page.

```javascript
$('#more_posts').bind( 'click', function(event){
    event.preventDefault();

    var location = window.location.pathname + "/" + $('.post-item')
        .size();

});
```

5. Now that we have the location, let's fill in the rest of the AJAX call. This time, we'll use the GET HTTP method and use the list of posts with the ID of post_list as our context, which will allow us to reference it in the success event. Then, let's just add a generic error event to let the user know something went wrong, if an error occurs.

```
$('#more_posts').bind( 'click', function(event){
  event.preventDefault();

  var location = window.location.pathname + "/" +
    $('#post_list').children().size();

  $.ajax({
    type: 'GET',
    url: location,
    context: $('#post_list'),
    success: function(html){
      // we'll fill this in, in just one second
    },
    error: function (request, status, error) {
      alert('An error occurred, please try again.');
    }
  });

});
```

6. Finally, let's fill in our success function with some code that appends the HTML returned from our AJAX call to the end of the post_list div. Then, we'll check to see if there are any other posts to load. If there are no more posts to load, we'll hide the **Load More** button. To get the number of posts, we're going to look at the span we created with post_count as an ID, and convert it to an integer with parseInt:

```
$('#more_posts').bind( 'click', function(event){
  event.preventDefault();

  var location = window.location.pathname + "/" +
    $('#post_list').children().size();

  $.ajax({
    type: 'GET',
    url: location,
    context: $('#post_list'),
    success: function(html){
      $(this).append(html);
```

```
    if ($('#post_list').children().size() <= "
      parseInt($('#post_count').text())) {
      $('#load_more').hide();
    }
  },
  error: function (request, status, error) {
    alert('An error occurred, please try again.');
  }
});

});
```

## What just happened?

In this section, we finished our pagination! We started by creating a quick CSS rule for our **Load More** link so that it looks a bit friendlier and added the HTML needed for it to appear on the profile page. We wrapped up the pagination by calling an AJAX function to the URL of the current user's profile and appended the number of posts that currently exist in `#post_list` div. By passing this number to our route, we're telling our route to pass the number along and to ignore all of those items, as we already have them displayed.

Next, we added a `success` function to return the HTML from our route using the layout of the `_posts` partial. This HTML will be appended at the end of the `#post_list` div. Finally, we checked to see if there were any more items to load by comparing the size of the `#post_list` against the number of posts our `reduce` function returned to the top of our profile in the `#post_count` span. If the two values are equal, it means that no more posts can be loaded, and we are safe to hide the **Load More** link.

## Time for action – fixing our delete post function to work with pagination

When we added the pagination, we also broke the ability to delete posts that are loaded via AJAX. This is because we are using the `bind` event handler to tie the `click` event to our links, which only happens on page load. So, we'll need to account for the links loaded via AJAX. Thankfully, we can do that using jQuery's `live` event handler.

*1.* Open `master.js`, and change the `delete` post code to use `live` instead of `bind`:

```
$('.delete').live( 'click', function(event){
  event.preventDefault();
  var location = $(this).attr('href');
```

2. If you start deleting a bunch of items in the post list, it currently doesn't change the number of posts tied to a user account using JavaScript. While we are here, let's alter the `success` function so that it also updates the number of posts at the top of our post list:

```
$('.delete').live( 'click', function(event){
  event.preventDefault();
  var location = $(this).attr('href');

  $.ajax({
    type: 'DELETE',
    url: location,
    context: $(this),
    success: function(html){
      $(this).parent().parent().parent().fadeOut();
      $('#post_count').text(parseInt($('#post_count').text()) -
        1);
    },
    error: function (request, status, error) {
      alert('An error occurred, please try again.');
    }
  });
});
```

## What just happened?

We just updated our delete button to use the `live` event handler instead of the `bind` event handler. By using `live`, jQuery allows us to define a selector and applies a rule to all current and future items that match that selector. Then, we made our `#post_count` element dynamic so that each time a post is deleted, the post count changes accordingly.

## Testing our complete pagination system

Our pagination is finally wrapped up. Let's go back and test everything to make sure that the pagination works as expected.

1. Go to `http://localhost/verge/login`, and log in to the application as `johndoe`.

2. Click on **My Profile**.

3. Scroll to the bottom of the page, and click on **Load More**. The next 10 posts will be returned to you.

4. If you have less than 20 posts in your account, the **Load More** button will disappear from the page, showing you that you have loaded all of the posts in your account.

5. Try and click on the last post in the list that was loaded through AJAX, and it will disappear, just as it should!

Amazing! Our pagination system works just as we wanted; we're able to delete posts, and our post count updates each time we delete a post.

# Using Gravatars

At this point, our profiles look a bit boring with just a bunch of text, because we don't have support for uploading images into our system. We're going to avoid this topic in this book for the sake of time, but also for our users' benefit. There is a decent amount of friction in getting users to upload a new profile image each time they join a service. Instead, there is a service that can make our lives a bit easier: **Gravatar** (http://www.gravatar.com). Gravatar is a web service that allows users to upload a profile image to one single location. From there, other applications can grab the profile image, using the user's e-mail address as the identifier of the image.

## Time for action – adding Gravatars to our application

Adding support for Gravatars through our user class is as easy as adding a few lines of code. After that, we'll add the gravatar function all over our application.

*1.* Open user/profile.php and a public function called gravatar that accepts a parameter called size; we'll give it a default value of 50.

```
public function gravatar($size='50') {

}
```

*2.* In order to get the users' Gravatar, we just need to create an md5 hash of a user's e-mail address, which will serve as the gravatar_id. We'll then set the size using our $size variable, and append all of that to Gravatar's web service URL.

```
public function gravatar($size='50') {
  return
    'http://www.gravatar.com/avatar/?gravatar_id='
    .md5(strtolower($this->email)).'&size='.$size;
}
```

**3.** That's it! We now have Gravatar support in our application. We just need to start adding it anywhere we want to see a profile image. Let's start by adding a large Gravatar into the **User Information** section at the top of the `views/user/profile.php` file.

```
<div class="span4">
  <div class="well sidebar-nav">
    <ul class="nav nav-list">
      <li><h3>User Information</h3></li>
      <li><img src="<?php echo $user->gravatar('100'); ?>" /></li>
      <li><b>Username:</b> <?php echo $user->name; ?></li>
      <li><b>Email:</b> <?php echo $user->email; ?></li>
    </ul>
  </div>
</div>
```

**4.** Next, let's update the listing of posts in the `views/user/_posts.php` file, so we can nicely display our Gravatars.

```
<?php foreach ($posts as $post): ?>
  <div class="post-item row">
    <div class="span7">
      <div class="span1">
        <img src="<?php echo $user->gravatar('50'); ?>" />
      </div>
      <div class="span5">
        <strong><?php echo $user->name; ?></strong>
        <p>
          <?php echo $post->content; ?>
        </p>
        <?php echo $post->date_created; ?>
      </div>
    </div>
    <div class="span1">
      <?php if ($is_current_user) { ?>
      <a href="<?php echo $this->make_route('/post/delete/' .
        $post->_id . '/' . $post->_rev)?>"
        class="deletes">(Delete)</a>
      <?php } ?>
    </div>
  <div class="span8"></div>
  </div>
<?php endforeach; ?>
```

## *What just happened?*

We added a function into our `User` class called `gravatar` that accepts a parameter of `$size` with a default value of `50`. From there, we made an `md5` hash of the object's e-mail address and `$size` and tacked it on to the end of Gravatar's web service. The result is a link to a nice and easy to display Gravatar image.

With our Gravatar system in place, we added it into our `views/user/profile.php` and `views/user/_posts.php` pages.

## Testing our Gravatars

Our Gravatars should be up and running on our profile page. If the user does not have an image tied to their e-mail address, a simple holding image will be shown.

1. Go to `http://localhost/user/johndoe`, and you will see Gravatar's placeholder on each post and in the **User Information** section.

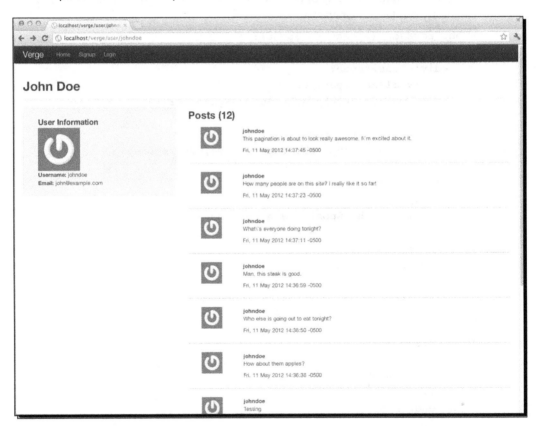

2. Now, let's associate a Gravatar with your e-mail by going to `http://www.gravatar.com` and clicking on **Sign up**.

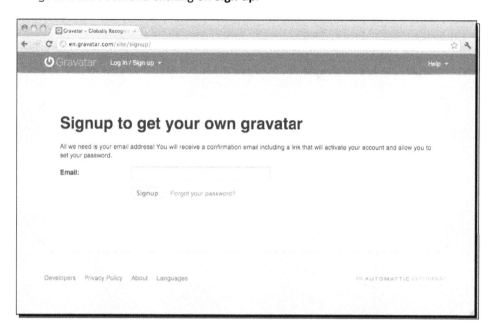

3. Type in your e-mail, and click on **Signup**. You'll receive a verification e-mail to your address, so go check it and click on the activation link.

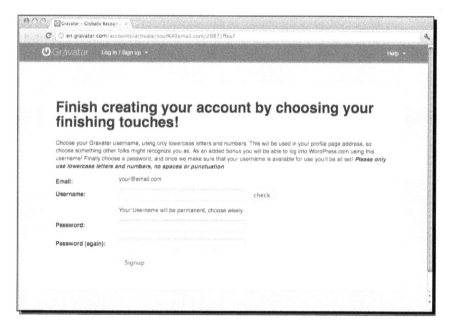

4.  Next, you will be taken to a page that shows your current account and images tied to your account. You will not have anything tied to your account yet, so click on **Add one by clicking here!**.

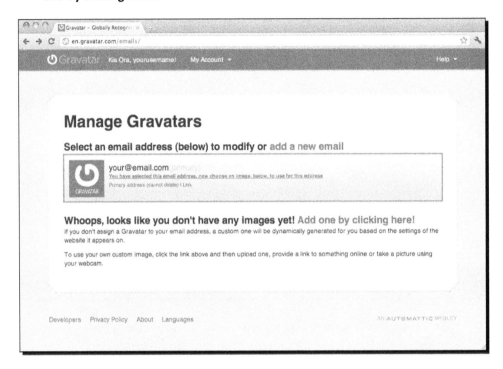

5.  After you have uploaded the image to the account and added any e-mail addresses you want to use, you can go back to the profile associated with your e-mail address (for me it's `http://localhost/user/tim`), and you will see a Gravatar in place!

## Adding everything to Git

I hope that in the course of this chapter, you've been committing your code to Git; if you haven't, this is your reminder. Make sure to do it early and often!

# Summary

I hope you enjoyed this chapter! While none of these features were "mission-critical" features for our application to work, these are the kinds of features that your users will request as your application grows.

Specifically, we learned how to install jQuery and use it to aid in the creation of some basic JavaScript and we used it to make the deletion of posts and pagination a bit cleaner. Next, we added Gravatar images to the profile and list of posts to make our profiles much more interesting to look at.

That's it! Our application is ready for prime time. In the next chapter, we're going to secure the final pieces of our application and deploy everything so that the world can see what you've built.

# 10
# Deploying your Application

*We have just a few more steps to complete before our application is live for the world to see and ready for users to sign up and create posts to their heart's content.*

We'll do the following things in this chapter to get our application up and running:

◆ We'll set up an account with Cloudant to house our application's CouchDB database and prepare it for our application

◆ We'll add a configuration class to our project to use environment variables to drive our application's settings

◆ We'll create an account with PHP Fog to host our application

◆ We'll configure Git to connect to PHP Fog's Git repository and deploy our application

As you might expect, we're going to be doing a lot of account setup and tweaking of our code in this chapter.

## Before we get started

For any application or database deployment, there are a variety of options for you. Each option has its strengths and weaknesses. I'd like to arm you with some knowledge instead of jumping right into setting up services, just in case you want to change to a different service some day.

In the past few years, Cloud has become one of the most used and abused terms in the technology industry. In order to completely understand the term Cloud, you'd have to read a whole lot of research papers and articles. But to keep it simple, the term **Cloud** describes the shift from the traditional single tenant approach with dedicated hosting, to a scalable, multi-tenant, and multi-platform host. CouchDB itself is a perfect example of a scalable database that could enable the Cloud architecture. Our application is also a good candidate for a Cloud solution, because we aren't storing anything locally, and we don't have any special dependencies for our application.

With that in mind, we're going to use Cloud services for both our application and database hosting. One of the added bonuses is that we'll be able to get our application up and running without paying a dime, and we'll only have to start paying as our application becomes successful. That's not a bad deal at all!

Let's quickly talk about how we'll approach our application and CouchDB hosting and the options that are available to us.

# Application hosting

When it comes to hosting web applications in the Cloud, there are a million ways it can be done. Since we aren't server setup geniuses, we'll want to use a high reward system that has a small amount of setup. With that in mind, we'll use **Platform as a Service (PaaS)**. There are quite a few PaaS solutions out there, but at this time, the best options for PHP developers are Heroku and PHP Fog.

**Heroku** (`http://www.heroku.com`) is the innovator that brought PaaS into the spotlight. They support PHP applications using their Cedar stack. But, because it's not a PHP-specific stack, it might be smarter for us to look to another provider.

**PHP Fog** (`http://www.phpfog.com`) is, in my opinion, a solid PaaS for developing PHP applications because of their very concentrated focus on PHP. They support a variety of PHP application frameworks out of the box, have MySQL hosting (if your application requires it), and in general, are geared towards providing a solid development environment, specifically for PHP developers.

With all of that in mind, PHP Fog is going to be the application hosting solution that we go with for this project.

# CouchDB hosting

There are far fewer solutions for CouchDB hosting than there are for application hosting, but luckily, they are all very solid products. The two services we'll talk about are Cloudant and IrisCouch.

**Cloudant** (`http://www.cloudant.com`) is one of the most robust solutions for CouchDB in the Cloud. They offer the familiar tools that we've used in this book, such as Futon and command-line, with the added ability to scale our data as it grows. Especially unique to Cloudant is that they offer custom solutions when your application requires some special functionality, and Cloudant is one of the larger contributors to CouchDB itself.

**Iris Couch** (`http://www.iriscouch.com`) also allows for free CouchDB hosting in the Cloud. Unfortunately, they just started to provide Couchbase server as their infrastructure, which is built on top of much of CouchDB's core. While I absolutely love Couchbase and its enhancements to the core CouchDB technology, we've been tasked with using only CouchDB for this book. But, if you find yourself in the market for Couchbase's enhanced functionality in the future, then it's definitely worth looking into Iris Couch.

Because I've used Cloudant in the past and know what it can handle, we'll use it for this project.

In general, the setup that we'll perform in this chapter is relatively similar to any of their competitive services. So, if you decide to switch later on, you should be well positioned to handle it without too many problems.

# Database hosting with Cloudant

In this section, we are going to set up a Cloudant server and prepare it for our application to connect to. There's very little setup to be done, and it will hopefully seem familiar to the steps we took early in the book when we set up our CouchDB databases.

# Getting started with Cloudant

Creating a Cloudant account is super easy, but let's walk through it just so that we're all on the same page.

1.  Start by going to `https://cloudant.com/sign-up/`, and you'll see the signup page.

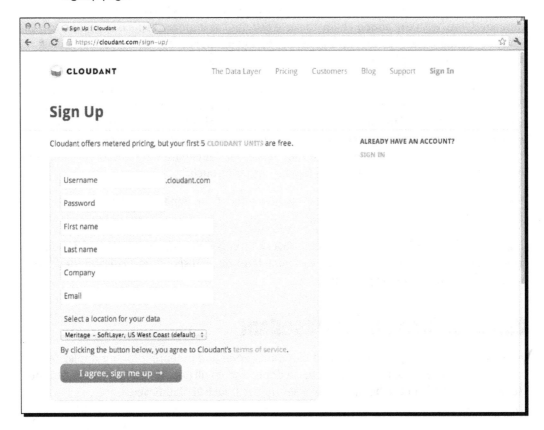

2.  Cloudant just needs some basic information to create your account. Start by entering a username. This will be used as your unique identifier and the link to your Cloudant account. I'd recommend picking something like your name or company name.

3.  Fill in the rest of the information on the page, and click the sign up button at the bottom of the page when you're ready!

You're all done, and you should be looking at your Cloudant dashboard. From here, you can manage your account and create new databases.

# Creating a _users database

We now have our brand new Cloudant account, but we don't have any databases yet. What's worse is that we don't even have our _users database. All we need to do is create a new _users database, and Cloudant will handle the rest. We technically could complete this process through Cloudant's interface, but let's use the command-line because it's a bit more universal.

1. Open Terminal.
2. Run the following command, and replace the two instances of username and the one instance of password, so that Cloudant knows who you are and what account you are trying to use:

   ```
   curl -X PUT https://username:password@username.cloudant.com/_users
   ```

   Terminal will let you know that your database has been created by returning you a success message:

   ```
   {"ok":true}
   ```

Great! Your _users database is now created. Remember that we also need another database called verge to store all of our data. Let's create the verge database next.

# Creating a verge database

You need to create another database in your account, this time calling it verge.

## Have a go hero – give it a shot yourself

Creating another database should be easy for you to do on your own now. Give it a shot by following the same steps we did while creating the _users database but changing the database name to verge instead.

If you feel stuck, I'll show you the command-line statement in just a moment. Okay, how'd it go? Let's recap the steps you needed to perform to create the verge database.

1. Open Terminal.
2. You should have ran the following command and replaced the two instances of username and the one instance of password, so that Cloudant would know who you are and what account you are trying to use:

   ```
   curl -X PUT https://username:password@username.cloudant.com/verge
   ```

   Terminal should have then reassured you that everything went okay when you saw a familiar success message, as follows:

   ```
   {"ok":true}
   ```

# Using Futon on Cloudant

Administrating the content from the command-line can be a bit tedious. Luckily, Cloudant also comes with our old friend – Futon. To get to Futon on Cloudant, follow these steps:

1.  Log in, and go to your dashboard.

2. Click on one of your database names; for this example, let's use verge.

This is the database detail page—as documents appear in your database, they will be displayed on this page.

3. Let's move on by clicking on the View in Futon button.

Look familiar? This is the same great Futon that we've been using locally.

# Configuring permissions

Now that we are live on our production database, it's incredibly important that we configure our permissions to work on our production server. If we don't secure our database, then our users could easily be readable, and that's not something we want to get tangled up in.

Luckily, Cloudant has taken care of all of these issues for us by doing the following:

- Because we've already created an account, the database is no longer in `Admin Party` mode
- By default, Cloudant makes the `_users` database administrable for our `admin` account, but no other accounts have access to it

We're lucky that Cloudant has our back! But, if you ever decide to roll out your own CouchDB instance, make sure to look back to *Chapter 3*, *Getting Started with CouchDB and Futon*, and follow the steps we took to secure our local environment.

We do, however, need to update our `verge` database so that users can read, create, and write in that database.

1. Log in to your Cloudant account, and go to your dashboard. `https://cloudant.com/#!/dashboard`.

2. Click on the `verge` database.

3. Click on **Permissions** to manage the database permissions.

4. Update the **Permissions** for **Everyone else** by checking the boxes under **Read**, **Create**, and **Write**. Make sure to leave **Admin** unchecked, so that normal users can't alter our database structure and design documents. The end result should look similar to the following screenshot:

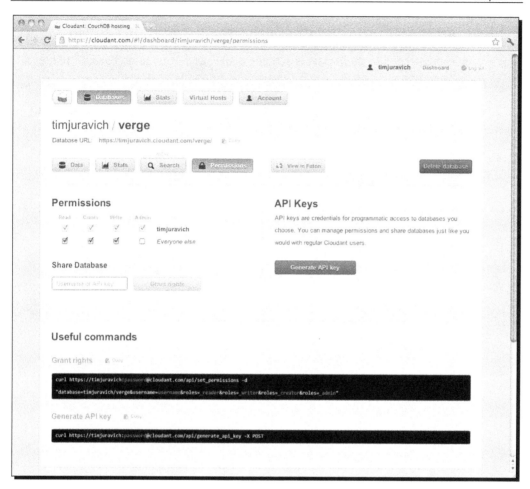

# Configuring our project

Now that we have our production database set up, our code needs to know how to connect to it. We could just alter over the hardcoded values we have in our `Bones` library and change it back and forth each time we want to develop locally or deploy to production. But, trust me that you don't want to go through the hassle of doing this, and more importantly, we don't want to store any usernames or passwords in our code; for this we'll use environment variables. **Environment variables** are a set of dynamically named values that allow you to define variables from the applications hosting environment. Let's create a class that will allow us to use environment variables so that our code is free of sensitive information and our application is easy to configure.

# Time for action – creating a configuration class

Plugging in a simple configuration class is actually really easy for us to do because of how we've coded everything so far. Let's walk through the creation of it together.

**1.** Start by creating a new configuration file called `configuration.php` inside our `lib` folder (`lib/configuration.php`).

**2.** Now, let's create the scaffolding for our class called `Configuration`.

```php
<?php

class Configuration {

}
```

**3.** Let's go through and create some descriptive configuration variables. We could add more, but let's just add the ones we need right now.

```php
<?php

class Configuration {

private $db_server = ';
private $db_port = '';
private $db_database = '';
private $db_admin_user = '';
private $db_admin_password = '';

}
```

**4.** Now, copy the login information you need to access your local CouchDB instance; mine looks similar to the following:

```php
<?php

class Configuration {

    private $db_server = '127.0.0.1';
    private $db_port = '5984';
    private $db_database = 'verge';
    private $db_admin_user = 'tim';
    private $db_admin_password = 'test';

}
```

**5.** Let's use a special __get function to check and see if there's an environment variable set, and return that instead of the default value. If not, it'll just return the default value that we define in this class.

```php
<?php

class Configuration {

  private $db_server = '127.0.0.1';
  private $db_port = '5984';
  private $db_database = 'verge';
  private $db_admin_user = 'tim';
  private $db_admin_password = 'test';

  public function __get($property) {
    if (getenv($property)) {
      return getenv($property);
    } else {
      return $this->$property;
    }
  }

}
```

## What just happened?

We just created a simple configuration class called `configuration.php` and created the shell of a class called `Configuration`. Next, we created a few variables for the configuration of the database, which we made `public` because we might need to use these variables in a variety of places. Then, we filled in the default values of these variables with the information to access our local CouchDB instance. We then added in the magic of this class. We created a __get function that overrides the standard `get` operation on a class. This function uses the `getenv` function to check the server to see if the variable is set in the environment variables (we'll go over how to do this shortly). If there is an environment variable with the same name, we'll return it to the calling function; if not, then we will simply return the default value.

The `Configuration` class is a nice and simple class that does everything we need without being overly complex. Next, let's move on to make sure that our application knows to access and use this class.

## Time for action – adding our configuration file to Bones

Adding the new configuration class to our application was pretty easy. Now, we just need to add it into our __construct() of Bones, and we should be able to start using this class throughout our project.

**1.** Open up lib/bones.php, and look at the beginning of the file where we tell our library where to look for our other lib files. We need to add our configuration class here.

```
require_once ROOT . '/lib/bootstrap.php';
require_once ROOT . '/lib/sag/src/Sag.php';
require_once ROOT . '/lib/configuration.php';
```

**2.** Let's make sure that we define $config in Bones' public variables so that we can use them in other files if we need to.

```
class Bones {
  private static $instance;
  public static $route_found = false;
  public $route = '';
  public $method = '';
  public $content = '';
  public $vars = array();
  public $route_segments = array();
  public $route_variables = array();
  public $couch;
  public $config;
```

**3.** Let's look at the __construct() method a bit further down in the file. In this method (right before the instantiation of Sag), let's create a new instance of the Configuration class.

```
public function __construct() {

  ...

  $this->config = new Configuration();
  $this->couch = new Sag('127.0.0.1','5984');
  $this->couch->setDatabase('verge');
}
```

**4.** Now that our code knows about the configuration class, we just need to put the variables in the right place and we'll be up and running. Let's tell Sag how to connect to CouchDB using the configuration class.

```
public function __construct() {
  $this->route = $this->get_route();
```

```
$this->route_segments = explode('/', trim($this->route, '/'));
$this->method = $this->get_method();

$this->config = new Configuration();
$this->couch = new Sag($this->config->db_server, $this->config-
>db_port);
$this->couch->setDatabase($this->config->db_database);
}
```

5.  There are just a few more places where we need to update our code, so that it uses the configuration class. Remember that we have the admin username and password in classes/user.php for the creation and finding of users. Let's clean this up by first looking at the signup function inside of classes/user.php. Once we plug in our configuration class, the function should look similar to the following:

```
public function signup($password) {
    $bones = new Bones();
    $bones->couch->setDatabase('_users');
    $bones->couch->login($bones->config->db_admin_user, $bones-
>config->db_admin_password);
```

6.  The last place that we need to adjust to use the config class is the get_by_ username function at the end of the classes/user.php file.

```
public static function get_by_username($username = null) {
    $bones = new Bones();
    $bones->couch->login($bones->config->db_admin_user, $bones-
>config->db_admin_password);
    $bones->couch->setDatabase('_users');
```

7.  We just removed all references to ADMIN_USER and ADMIN_PASSWORD, which we defined at the top of index.php. We no longer need these variables, so let's switch over to index.php and remove both ADMIN_USER and ADMIN_PASSWORD from the top of the file.

## What just happened?

We just wrote the final lines of code of our application! In this section, we made sure that Bones had complete access to the configuration file that we recently created as lib/configuration.php. Then, we made a public variable, $config, to make sure that we had access to our configuration class anywhere in our application. With our configuration class stored in the $config variable, we moved on to go through places in our code where we hardcoded our database settings.

# Adding changes to Git

Because we just wrote the last lines of our code, I'm going to be a pain and will make sure that you've fully committed all of our code to Git. Otherwise, when we deploy our code shortly, there's a chance that not all of your files will make it to the production server.

1.  Open Terminal.

2.  Add any remaining files in your project using the wildcard.

    ```
    git add .
    ```

3.  Now, let's tell Git what we have done.

    ```
    git commit -m 'Abstracted out environment specific variables into
    lib/configuration.php and preparing for launch of our site 1.0!'
    ```

# Application hosting with PHP Fog

Our code is all up-to-date and ready to be deployed. We just need a place to actually deploy it. As I mentioned before, we will use PHP Fog, but feel free to explore the other options that are available to you. The setup and deploy process will be the same with most PaaS providers.

## Setting up a PHP Fog account

Setting up a PHP Fog account is just as easy as it was for us to set up our Cloudant account.

1.  Start by going to `https://www.phpfog.com/signup`.

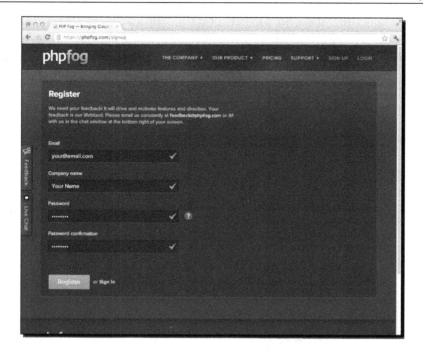

2. Create an account by filling in each field. When you are finished, click on **Register**. You'll be forwarded on to create your first app.

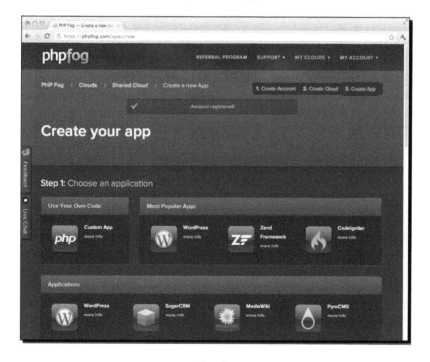

3. You'll notice that there are a variety of starter applications and frameworks that allow us to jump in and create the scaffolding of a PHP application. We're just going to use our own code, so click on **Custom App**.

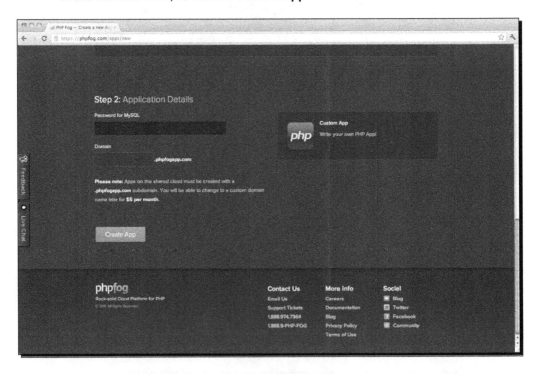

4. Our application is almost created, we just need to give PHP Fog a bit more information.

5. You'll notice that PHP Fog is asking for a password for MySQL. Since we aren't using MySQL in this application, we can just enter a random password or any other characters. It is helpful to know that some day down the road, if you'd like to use MySQL in your project to store some relational data, it's just a few clicks away and hosted in the same application environment. Remember that MySQL and CouchDB can be the best of friends if you use them right!

6. Next, PHP Fog will ask for your domain. Each application will have a short URL hosted on phpfogapp.com. This is totally fine for us in the short term, and when we're ready to roll out our application with a full domain name, we can do that through PHP Fog's **Domain Name** section. When creating a domain for your application, PHP Fog requires it to be unique, so you'll need to come up with your own domain. You could do something like yourname-verge.phpfogapp.com, or you can get especially clever and create an app with the name of your favorite mythological creature. This is a popular practice, so that nobody can randomly find your application while you're still fixing bugs and getting ready to launch.

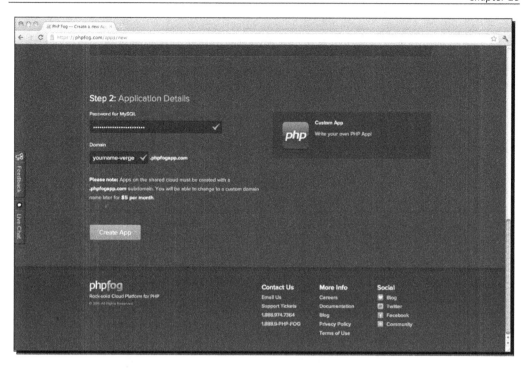

7. When you are ready, click on **Create App**, and your application will be created.

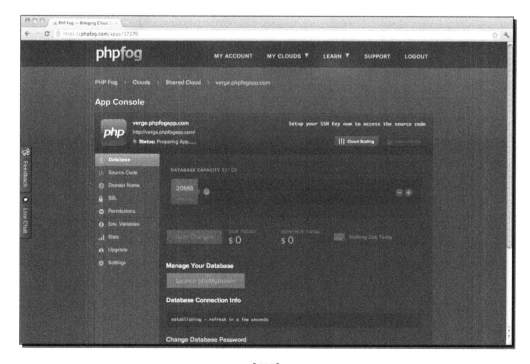

8. That's all it takes! Your application is getting ready to start. You'll notice that PHP Fog will say **Status: Preparing App...** for just a few moments, and then it will change to **Status: Running**.

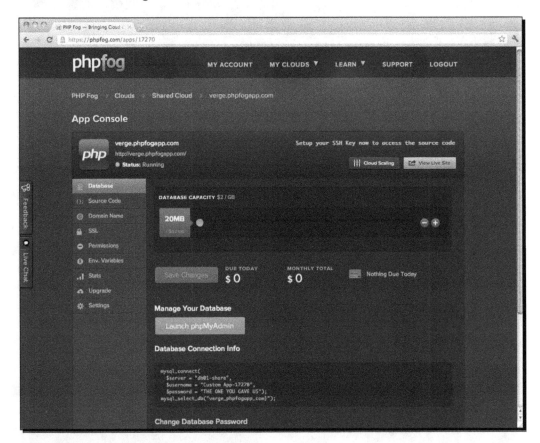

# Creating environment variables

With our PHP Fog application up and running, we have one last piece of configuration that we need to carry out before pushing our code to the server. Remember all of the environment variables we set up when configuring your project? Well, we need to set them within PHP Fog so that our application knows how to connect to Cloudant.

In order for you to manage your environment variables, you'll need to start by navigating to your **App Console** for your project, which is where we left off after you created your first app.

Click on **Env Variables**, and you will be taken to the **Environment Variables management** section.

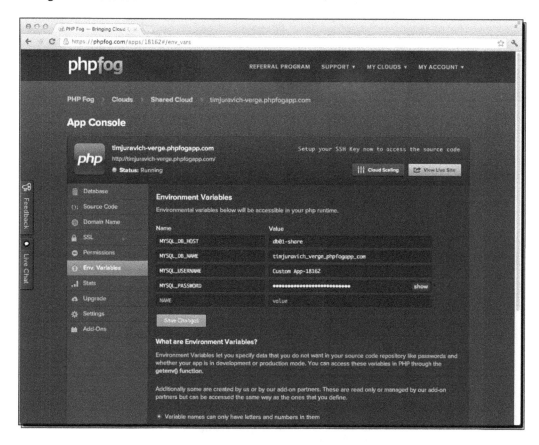

You'll notice that the environment variables for the MySQL database that PHP Fog created for us are already set. We just need to enter in our environment variables for Cloudant. The name will need to be the same name that we defined in our configuration class earlier in this chapter.

Let's start by adding our `db_server` environment variable. My `db_server` is located at `https://timjuravich:password@timjuravich.cloudant.com`, so I'll enter those details into the **Name** and **Value** text fields.

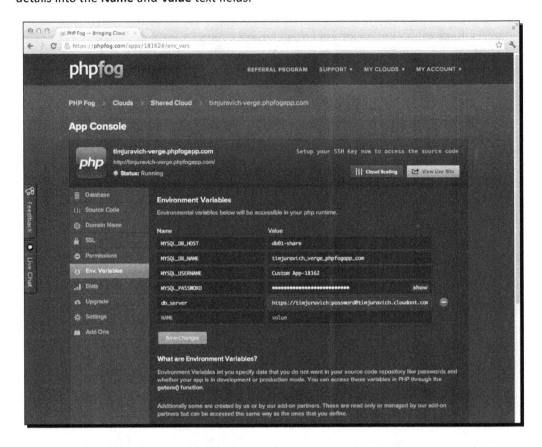

Let's continue this process for each of the variables inside of the configuration file. To recap, here are the environment variables that you'll need to enter here:

- `db_server`: This will be your Cloudant URL, again, mine is `https://timjuravich:password@timjuravich.cloudant.com`

- `db_port`: This is will be set to `5984`

- `db_database`: This is the database where everything will be stored, and it should be set to `verge`

- `db_admin_user`: This is the username of the `admin` user. In our case, this is set to the value of the Cloudant admin username

- `db_admin_password`: This is the password for the above `admin` user

When you are all finished, click on **Save Changes**, and your environment variables will be set. With that, we're ready to deploy to PHP Fog.

# Deploying to PHP Fog

Deploying to PHP Fog is an extremely simple process, because PHP Fog uses Git for deployments. It's a good thing that our project is already set up with Git and ready to go. We just need to tell PHP Fog our SSH key, so that it knows how to identify us.

## Adding our SSH key to PHP Fog

PHP Fog uses SSH keys just like GitHub to identify and authenticate us. Since we already created one early in this book, we don't need to make another one.

1. You can start by clicking on **MY ACCOUNT** in the top-right corner and then clicking on **SSH Key** on the next page. You'll be presented with the following page in which you can enter your SSH key:

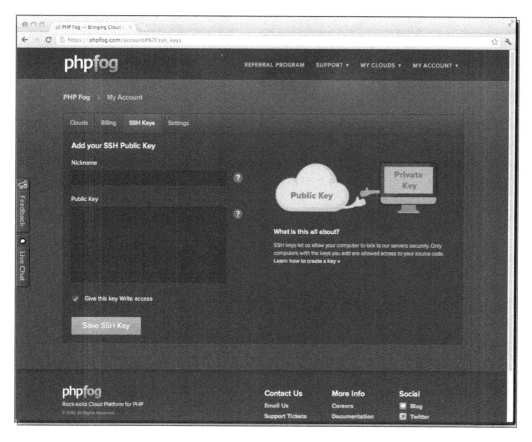

2.  Enter a value for **Nickname**. You should use something simple but descriptive, such as `Tim's Macbook`. You'll thank yourself later for keeping this organized, especially if you start to collaborate with other developers on this project.

    You'll need to grab your public key for the **Public Key** textbox. Luckily, we can do that with one simple command in Terminal.

3.  Open Terminal.

4.  Run the following command, and your public key will be copied to your clipboard.

    ```
    pbcopy< ~/.ssh/id_rsa.pub
    ```

5.  With the public key in your clipboard, just click on the textbox and paste in the value.

6.  Finally, at the bottom of the form, there's a checkbox that says **Give this key Write access**. If you want the computer to be able to push the code to PHP Fog (which we'll want to be able to do), this needs to be checked.

7.  Click on **Save SSH Key**, and we're ready to move on to the final steps of deploying our application.

## Connecting to PHP Fog's Git repository

As we already have our Git repository all set up and ready to go, all we need to do is tell Git how to connect to the repository on PHP Fog. Let's go through this process by adding a remote repository to our working directory called `phpfog`.

### Get the repository from Php Fog

When we created our application on PHP Fog, we also created a unique Git repository that our application is driven by. In this section, we'll grab the location of this repository, so that we can tell Git to connect to it.

1.  Log in to your PHP Fog Account.

2.  Go to your application's App Console.

3.  Click on **Source Code**.

4.  On the **Source Code** page, you'll see a section that says **Clone your git repository**. Mine has the following code in it (yours should be similar):

    ```
    git clone git@git01.phpfog.com:timjuravich-verge.phpfogapp.com
    ```

5.  Because we already have an existing Git repository, we don't have to clone theirs, but we do need the location of the application's Git repository for our next configuration step. Using this example, the repository location would be `git@git01.phpfog.com:timjuravich-verge.phpfogapp.com`. Copy this to your clipboard.

## Connecting to the repository from Git

Now that we know our PHP Fog's Git repository, we just need to tell our local machine how to connect to it.

1. Open Terminal.

2. Change the directory to your `working` folder.

   ```
   cd /Library/WebServer/Documents/verge
   ```

3. Now, let's add our PHP Fog's repository as a new remote repository called `phpfog`.

   ```
   git remote add phpfog git@git01.phpfog.com:verge.phpfogapp.com
   ```

4. Clear the runway, and we're ready to launch this application!

# Deploy to PHP Fog

It's the moment we've been waiting for! Let's launch our application to PHP Fog.

1. Open Terminal.

2. Change the directory to your `working` folder.

   ```
   cd /Library/WebServer/Documents/verge
   ```

3. We want to ignore what's in PHP Fog's Git repository, as we already have our application built. So, this time and this time only, we'll want to append `--force` at the end of our call.

   ```
   git push origin master --force
   ```

I hope that wasn't too anti-climactic, but congratulations, your application is live to the world! That was nice and easy wasn't it? Each time you make changes to your code from here on out, all you need to do is commit it to Git, enter the command `git push phpfog master`, and make sure to push your code to GitHub too by using `git push origin master`.

If you start to play with your live application a bit, you might be bummed to find out that your data from your local machine isn't up for you to see. You're in luck; in the next section, we're going to push our local database to our production database using CouchDB's powerful replication.

# Replicating local data to production

The inner workings and background info on replication won't be covered in detail in this section, but you can find a full walkthrough in the bonus chapter titled *Replicating your data*, which is available on the Packt Publishing website.

To give you a quick overview, **replication** is the way that CouchDB transports data between one server and another. Replication is driven by the `_rev` field that lives in each document, the `_rev` field makes sure that your server knows which version has the correct data to use.

In this section, we'll replicate both the `_users` and `verge` databases so that all of our local data is available on the production server. You don't have to worry if your application has been live for a few minutes or even a few days, as the best part of replication is that if someone is already using your application, then all of their data will remain intact; we'll just be adding our local data.

## Time for action – replicating our local _users database to Cloudant

Let's use Futon to replicate our local `_users` database to the `_users` database that we created on Cloudant.

*1.* Open Futon in the browser and click on **Replicator**, or you can navigate directly to `http://localhost:5984/_utils/replicator.html`.

*2.* Make sure that you are signed in as the `administrator`; if you are not, click on **Login** and sign in as an `administrator`.

*3.* Select the `_users` database in the **Replicate changes from** the dropdown list.

**4.** Click on the **Remote database** radio button in the **To** section.

5. In the **Remote database** text field, enter the URL of the database at Cloudant along with the credentials. The format of the URL will look similar to `https://username:password@username.cloudant.com/_users`.

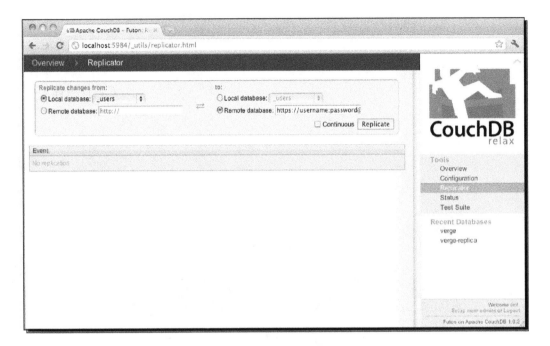

6. Click on **Replicate**, and CouchDB will push your local database to Cloudant.

**7.** You'll see the familiar results from Futon.

## What just happened?

We just used Futon to replicate our local _users database to our _users production database hosted with Cloudant. The process was exactly the same as we've done before, however, we used **Remote Database** in the **To** section, and used the URL of the database along with our credentials. When replication was complete, we received a long and confusing report, but the gist of it is that that everything went okay. Let's move on to replicating our verge database as well.

> It's worth mentioning that if you attempted to replicate the _users database from the command-line, you would have had to include the username and password in your call. This is because we have the users database completely locked to anonymous users. The function would look similar to the following:
>
> curl -X POST http://user:password@localhost:5984/_replicate -d '{"source":"_users", "target":"https://username:password@username.cloudant.com/_users"}' -H "Content-Type: application/json"

### Have a go hero – replicating the local verge database to Cloudant

Do you think you can figure out the command to replicate your local verge database to the verge database on Cloudant based on the tip I just gave you? It's almost impossible to mess anything up at this stage in the game, so don't be scared to try a few things if you don't get it the first time.

Give it a shot. When you're finished, continue reading and we'll go over the command that I used.

How did everything go? Hopefully, you got it without too much effort. If you couldn't get it to work, here's an example of a command you could have used:

```
curl -X POST http://user:password@localhost:5984/_replicate -d
'{"source":"verge","target":"https://username:password@username
.cloudant.com/verge"}' -H "Content-Type: application/json"
```

In this example, we're using our local CouchDB instance to replicate our local verge database to the target Cloudant verge database. For the local database, we can simply put the name as verge, but for the target database, we have to pass the full database location.

With all of your data live and on your production server, you can log in as any of the users that you created locally, and see all of the content that you created live and ready for the world to see. This it's not quite the end of your journey; let's talk quickly about what's next.

# What's next?

Before I send you on your way, let's talk about what's in store for you with your application in the wild, and what you can do next to make this application more powerful.

## Scaling your application

Luckily, scaling your application should be really easy when leveraging PHPFog and Cloudant. Really, the most intense thing you'll have to do is log in to PHPFog and bump up our web processes, or log in to Cloudant and upgrade to a bigger plan. They handle all of the hard work; you just need to learn how to scale effectively. You can't beat that!

For more information on how to scale effectively, browse the help documents of both PHPFog and Cloudant, they talk a lot of about different ways that you can scale and problem areas to avoid.

It's worth mentioning again that we didn't fully cover replication in this chapter. For a full walkthrough of replication, be sure to checkout the bonus chapter titled *Replicating your data*, which is available on the Packt Publishing website.

## Next steps

I hope that you continue to develop and adapt Verge into something supremely useful, or if not, I hope you take the knowledge learned in this book and build something much greater.

If you decide to keep building features on top of Verge, there's still quite a lot that you could do with this application. For example, you could:

- Add the ability for users to follow other users
- Allow users to filter and search content
- Add a messaging system so users can communicate with each other
- Customize the UI and make it into something really unique

I will continue to incrementally add features like these and more to the Verge repository on GitHub here: `https://github.com/timjuravich/verge`. So, make sure to watch the repository for updates, and fork it if you'd like.

Again, I really appreciate the time we spent together in this book, please feel free to reach out to me on Twitter `@timjuravich` if you have any questions.

Happy developing!

# Summary

In this chapter, we learned how to share our application with the world. Specifically, we signed up for an account with Cloudant and PHP Fog, and deployed our application successfully. All that's left for you to do is keep coding and turn this application into something awesome.

# Pop Quiz Answers

## Chapter 2, Setting up your Development Environment

| 1 | When we are using the default Apache installation for web developing, where is the default working directory? | `[/Library/WebServer/Documents]` |
|---|---|---|
| 2 | In order to use our local development environment with CouchDB, we need to make sure that two services are running. What are they, and how do you make them run in Terminal? | ◆ [Apache]<br>`sudo apachetl start`<br>◆ [CouchDB]<br>`couchdb -b` |
| 3 | What command line statement do you use to issue a Get request to CouchDB? | `curl http://127.0.0.1:5984/` |

# Chapter 3, Getting Started with CouchDB and Futon

| | | |
|---|---|---|
| **1** | What is the first sentence of CouchDB's definition according to `http://couchdb.apache.org/`? | CouchDB is a document database server, accessible through the RESTful JSON API. |
| **2** | What are the four verbs used by HTTP, and how does each match up to CRUD? | ◆  `[GET -> Read]`<br>◆  `[PUT -> Create, Update]`<br>◆  `[POST -> Create]`<br>◆  `[DELETE -> Delete]` |
| **3** | What is the URL to access Futon? | `http://localhost:5984/_utils/` |
| **4** | What does the term Admin Party mean to CouchDB, and how do you take CouchDB out of this mode? | The term Admin Party is the default state of CouchDB where there are no server admins, therefore there are no restrictions on users.<br><br>By clicking on **Fix This** and adding a server admin, we can take CouchDB out of this mode. |
| **5** | How would you authenticate a user for a secure database through the command-line? | By prepending `username:password@` to the URL |

# Index

_sum, reduce function 201
_users database 127
_users database, Cloudant
    creating 246

# A

ACID
    about 10
    properties 10
ACID, properties
    atomicity 10
    consistency 10
    durability 10
    isolation 10
action attribute 76
administrator setup 127
ADMIN_PASSWORD constant 133
ADMIN_USER constant 133
AJAX
    using, to delete posts 220-222
alerts
    showing 143-145
answers
    pop quiz 273, 274
Apache
    about 20
    configuration 25, 26
    fine tuning 25
    installing, on Linux 17
    installing, on Windows 16
Apache's error log
    examining 139, 140
Apache's log, user profile
    examining 160, 161
API 38
application
    Gravatars, adding 234, 235
    stylesheet, creating 85
    support adding, to consume reduce function
        204-206
application hosting
    Heroku 242
    PHP Fog 242, 256
    Platform as a Service (PaaS) 242

Application Programming Interface. *See* API
atomicity, ACID property 10

# B

Base object
    about 111
    creating 107-109
bind event handler 232
bones
    about 54
    allowing, to store content path 68, 69
    allowing, to store variables 68, 69
    application, hooking up to 60
    class structure, creating 61
    configuration file, adding 254, 255
    helpers, adding 75
    Sag, adding 104, 105
    simple layout file, creating 70
    skeleton, creating 59
    using, to handle requests 60
bones class
    about 61
    get function, creating 64
Boostrap's JavaScript files
    connecting 218, 219
Bootstrap
    about 115
    home page, sprucing up 120
    including 118, 119
    local installation 116, 117
    user files, moving to user folder 122
    user views, organizing 122

# C

CAP theorem
    about 9
    avialability 10
    consistency 10
    partition-tolerance 10
Cascading Style Sheets (CSS) 55
catch block 148
classes directory
    adding 107
    working with 107

**Linux**
Apache, installing  17
CouchDB, installing  17
Git, installing  17
PHP, installing  17
**local data**
replicating, to production  266
**local _users database**
replicating, to Cloudant  266-270
**local verge database**
replicating, to Cloudant  270, 271
**LoveSeat  215**

# M

**magic methods  109**
**make_input function  129**
**map function**
about  185-187
querying  193, 194
**Map Function text area  188**
**MapReduce  206**
**master.css  85**
**master.js**
Boostrap's JavaScript files, connecting  218, 219
creating  218, 219
**Membase  13**
**message variable  94**
**MySQL**
posts, modeling  174

# N

**name field  46, 123**
**National Security Agency (NSA)  134**
**newDoc  211**
**NoSQL  8, 34**
**NoSQL database**
advantages  11
classifying  8, 9
column stores  8
disadvantages  11
document stores  9
evolution  7
graph databases  9
key-value stores  8

stages, for avoiding  12
uses  11

# O

**oldDoc  211**

# P

**PaaS  242**
**password_sha field  123**
**PHP**
about  22
Apache connection, testing  23
CouchDB document, creating with  98-102
quick info page, creating  23-25
version, checking  22
**PHP Fog**
about  242
account, setting up  256-260
application, hosting with  256
deploying to  263, 265
environment variables, creating  260-263
Git repository, connecting to  264
repository connecting to, from Git  265
repository, getting  264
SSH key, adding  263, 264
URL  242
**Platform as a Service.** *See* **PaaS**
**pop quiz**
answers  273, 274
**post class**
setting up  176, 177
**post method  76**
**posts**
about  174
adding, to user profile  198, 199
changes, adding to Git  182, 183
creating  177
creation enabling, by making form  178, 179
creation handling, by creating function  177, 178
deleting AJAX used, to improve user experience  220-222
deleting, support adding for  208, 209

user object, creating 109, 110

user object, plugging 111

**SagCouchException**

used, for handling document update conflicts 142

**SagCouchException. SagCouchException class 140**

**salt 134**

**salt field 124**

**security**

_users database, accessing 47-49

about 46

CouchDB, removing 46, 47

database security, checking 50, 51

**session_start 150**

**session_write_close 149**

**set function 69**

**SHA-1 134**

**signup function 141**

**signup process**

about 126

administrator setup 127

cleaning up 136, 137

interface, updating 127-130

refactoring 136

SHA-1 134, 135

simple user signup, handling 130-134

testing 135

**signup script**

code, committing to 102

code, committing to Git 97

CouchDB document, creating with curl 98-102

CouchDB document, creating with PHP 98-102

data posting to CouchDB, curl calls used 95

e-mail field, adding 95

logic, adding 94

standard object, creating for JSON encoding 96

**simple pagination**

adding, jQuery used 223

backend support, adding 225

code, refactoring 228, 229

delete post function, fixing 232, 233

frontend support, adding 230, 231

pagination system, testing 233

**simple user signup, signup process**

handling 130-134

**single user documents, user profile**

getting 156, 157

**Singleton Pattern 61**

**SQL SELECT statement 186**

**SSH key, PHP Fog**

adding 263, 264

**static:get_instance() function 63**

**strtolower function 107**

**submit button 76**

**success event 231**

**success function 232, 233**

**success: function() 222**

**success option 221**

**success variable 222**

# T

**tail command 140**

**temporary view**

creating 187-189

**terminal**

about 18

using, to show hidden files 19

**test-db database 41**

**text editor 20**

**The _id 186**

**to_json function 207**

**to_json() function 111**

**try catch statement 141**

**type: 'DELETE' 221**

**type field 124**

# U

**url: location 221**

**user authentication**

about 145

current user, handling 151-153

forms for login, setting up 145, 146

logging in 147

logging out 147

login form, setting up 145

log in functionality, adding for users 147-149

log out functionality, adding for users  150

routes for login, setting up  145, 146

**userCtx  211**

**user document, CouchDB**

about  123

designing  123

e-mail field  124

fields, adding  124

fields, adding to support  125

full name field  124

_id field  123

name field  123

options, for adding field  124

password_sha field  123

_rev field  123

roles field  124

salt field  124

support, adding for additional fields  125

type field  124

username field  124

**user experience**

improving, by using AJAX to delete posts  220-222

**user files**

moving, to user folder  122

**user folder**

user files, moving to  122

**User-Generated Content.** *See* **UGC**

**user log in, user profile**

checking  171, 172

**username field  124**

**user object  111**

**user profile**

404 errors, displaying  166

404 errors, displaying for unknown users  167, 168

404 errors, handling with bones  167-169

404 errors, testing  169, 170

500 errors, handling  162

500 errors, handling with bones  162

about  155

Apache's log, examining  160, 161

changes, adding to Git  159, 174

creating, steps for  158, 159

design, cleaning up  172

errors, finding  160

exception handler, testing  165, 166

exceptions, handling  163, 165

issues, fixing  160

link, giving to profile  170, 171

new profile, checking up  173, 174

posts, adding  198, 199

route, creating for  157, 158

single user documents, getting  156, 157

testing  159

user log in, checking  171, 172

**users_groups  34**

**user views**

organizing  122

# V

**validate_doc_update function  212, 213**

**validate function  211**

adding  211-213

**validation, design documents**

$_rev, support adding for  207

about  206

CouchDB's support  210, 211

delete buttons, hiding  214

posts deleting, support adding for  208, 209

validate function, adding  211

**validation function  207**

**verge**

about  53

database creating, cUrl used  94

directories, creating  54, 55

**verge database  206**

**verge database, Cloudant**

creating  246

**verge_user  124**

**version control**

about  31

Git  31

Git, configuring  31

Git, installing  31

**views**

adding, to application  70

## Thank you for buying
## CouchDB and PHP Web Development  Beginner's Guide

## About Packt Publishing

Packt, pronounced 'packed', published its first book "*Mastering phpMyAdmin for Effective MySQL Management*" in April 2004 and subsequently continued to specialize in publishing highly focused books on specific technologies and solutions.

Our books and publications share the experiences of your fellow IT professionals in adapting and customizing today's systems, applications, and frameworks. Our solution based books give you the knowledge and power to customize the software and technologies you're using to get the job done. Packt books are more specific and less general than the IT books you have seen in the past. Our unique business model allows us to bring you more focused information, giving you more of what you need to know, and less of what you don't.

Packt is a modern, yet unique publishing company, which focuses on producing quality, cutting-edge books for communities of developers, administrators, and newbies alike. For more information, please visit our website: www.packtpub.com.

## About Packt Open Source

In 2010, Packt launched two new brands, Packt Open Source and Packt Enterprise, in order to continue its focus on specialization. This book is part of the Packt Open Source brand, home to books published on software built around Open Source licences, and offering information to anybody from advanced developers to budding web designers. The Open Source brand also runs Packt's Open Source Royalty Scheme, by which Packt gives a royalty to each Open Source project about whose software a book is sold.

## Writing for Packt

We welcome all inquiries from people who are interested in authoring. Book proposals should be sent to author@packtpub.com. If your book idea is still at an early stage and you would like to discuss it first before writing a formal book proposal, contact us; one of our commissioning editors will get in touch with you.

We're not just looking for published authors; if you have strong technical skills but no writing experience, our experienced editors can help you develop a writing career, or simply get some additional reward for your expertise.

## Cassandra High Performance Cookbook

ISBN: 978-1-84951-512-2      Paperback: 310 pages

Over 150 recipes to design and optimize large-scale Apache Cassandra deployments

1. Get the best out of Cassandra using this efficient recipe bank

2. Configure and tune Cassandra components to enhance performance

3. Deploy Cassandra in various environments and monitor its performance

4. Well illustrated, step-by-step recipes to make all tasks look easy!

## PHP and MongoDB Web Development Beginner's Guide

ISBN: 978-1-84951-362-3      Paperback: 292 pages

Combine the power of PHP and MongoDB to build dynamic web 2.0 applications

1. Learn to build PHP-powered dynamic web applications using MongoDB as the data backend

2. Handle user sessions, store real-time site analytics, build location-aware web apps, and much more, all using MongoDB and PHP

3. Full of step-by-step instructions and practical examples, along with challenges to test and improve your knowledge

Please check **www.PacktPub.com** for information on our titles

## PHP jQuery Cookbook

ISBN: 978-1-84951-274-9        Paperback: 332 pages

Over 60 simple but highly effective recipes to create interactive web applications using PHP with jQuery

1. Create rich and interactive web applications with PHP and jQuery

2. Debug and execute jQuery code on a live site

3. Design interactive forms and menus

4. Another title in the Packt Cookbook range, which will help you get to grips with PHP as well as jQuery

## PHP Ajax Cookbook

ISBN: 978-1-84951-308-1        Paperback: 340 pages

Over 60 simple but incredibly effective recipes to Ajaxify PHP websites

1. Learn how to develop and deploy iPhone web and native apps

2. Optimize the performance of Ajax applications

3. Build dynamic websites with faster response from the server using the asynchronous call feature of PHP Ajax

4. Using Ajax allows quick and efficient access of data from the server, thus precluding a total web page refresh

Please check **www.PacktPub.com** for information on our titles